The Effective Woman Manager

The Effective Woman Manager

Seven Vital Skills for Upward Mobility

NATHANIEL STEWART

Director, Institute for Women in Management

A Wiley-Interscience Publication
JOHN WILEY & SONS, New York • Chichester • Brisbane • Toronto

Library of Congress Cataloging in Publication Data:

Stewart, Nathaniel, 1912-
　　The effective woman manager.

　　"A Wiley-Interscience publication."
　　Bibliography: p.
　　1. Women executives.　2. Women in business.
3. Management.　I. Title.

HF5500.2.S73　　　　658.4'002'4042　　　　77-28277
ISBN 0-471-04148-3

Printed in the United States of America

10　9　8　7　6　5　4

To my wife Amelia who managed it all with skill and dedication

. . . from Nashville to New Orleans, from Washington
    to New York, and all other routes on the journey together.

Foreword

What do you do if you are a woman with ability and aspirations, eager to move up in management? Even for men, and especially for women, the path is vast and complicated. Yet one should be able to get help somewhere. This book is *clearly* such a valuable source of help to you.

Today a woman really has an extra advantage. Management conscience, the need for competent managers in a fast-moving and competitive world, and pressures from government have all provided this special edge for the woman with the will and the intelligence to succeed. Since there are still very few women in management, and fewer still who can really write about it, one turns to the existing sources, mostly men with expertise in management, considerable experience in educating and training managers, and extensive writing in the field. The author of this book comes with these assets, and the special experience of having worked with women managers.

Very few writers have focused on the special role that women can play. When they do, unfortunately, it is often with tongue in cheek or a condescending approach. Dr. Stewart, by contrast, talks to us honestly, with keen insight and a special grasp for our problems, skills, and possibilities as women.

If you are a woman you will enjoy and benefit from this straightforward approach to such issues as dealing with your peers (primarily men), delegating and coordinating with others, and really administering. If you are a man, you will gain insight from the concepts and vital skills discussed, and especially from the issues raised about woman manager relationships.

It is with thanks and pleasure that I recommend this clear and well developed guide for the woman finding her way in the complicated world of management. A special recommendation to many of my women friends, but also to the myriad of male colleagues in management who have taught me many of the skills and techniques that Dr. Stewart so ably discusses.

EDITH M. LYNCH
Vice President—Manager
Personnel Division
National Retail Merchants Association

Preface

A mariner does not navigate in rough waters without a log book and a compass. Similarly, one does not casually "ship out" on the turbulent waters of women's rights, opportunities, and roles in contemporary society. Women in management are clearly part of these issues, as the many useful but often emotional round tables, conferences, and seminars attest. But they need guidance about the routes, the hazards, and the expectations of managerial life.

What is the path to effective disciplined performance for the woman manager? Whatever label you use—knowledge, judgment, aptitudes, skills, abilities, outlook, attitudes, education—they must ultimately yield one outcome: her competence to produce results that benefit the organization. As Virginia Trotter, assistant secretary of the Department of Health, Education, and Welfare, has said:

> A woman must be *competent* in whatever she decides to do because opportunity means nothing if we're not prepared to take advantage of it.

Constance Smolowe, in her *Corporations and Women,* puts it realistically:

> The key to women's rise to power in the nation's corporations seems to lie not in . . . inspirational exhortations, but in the ability to

translate equality into the thing corporations understand best: profits.*

And profits are attained through successful management of an
organization by a competent team of professionals—directors,
managers, and supervisors who lead the corps of skilled employees.

This book deals with the components that the new or inexperienced—or experienced—woman manager must master to show her
ability to cope with the four R's—role, risks, relationships, results.
Proven competency to deal with these is the test. It seeks, more
specifically, (1) to *accelerate the pace* at which the woman manager
masters the skills that earn earlier recognition and advancement; (2)
to help her work constructively and productively in a *peer relationship* with all managers (past prejudices and wounds notwithstand-
ing); (3) to see *assertiveness as an asset* in getting things done, not
the intimidating trait of the stereotyped female supervisor; (4) to
concentrate on a set of seven *vital managerial skills* that can
"make" the woman manager; and (5) to stress her incumbency as a
line manager rather than a staff specialist wherever possible, since
this is where she has been most deprived of opportunity in a male
business culture. To give the book any other rationale would only
create an ersatz Betty Friedan tract or Margaret Mead treatise, or
another conventional textbook on the principles of management.

The focus of this book is the individual with present or future responsibilities in middle management. There is no particular mystique about this category. It does, however, embrace many
echelons often seen as management levels. To deal merely with
first-line supervision would be perfunctory and a further denial of
status to the career woman—however, important experiences at the
first-line supervisory level may be *en route* to higher levels. To deal
with top-level executive content would be unrealistic, since less than
2 percent of women are now in such positions. Moreover, the very

---

*From Constance Smolowe, "Corporations and Women." *MBA Magazine,*
February 1974. Reprinted with permission of *MBA Magazine.* Copyright © 1974 by
MBA Communications, Inc.

nature of certain problems and events discussed in this book often involve "spill-over" from one echelon to another.

Certain skills or functions that are generally recognized as essential in management—directing, motivating, leading, and controlling, for example—are not treated in isolation, but are woven into the broader discussions. Similarly, topics like MBO (management by objectives), OD (organizational development), and MIS (management information systems) are not treated in themselves. And for obvious reasons: the well-motivated, aspiring woman manager, like many men, will be a serious, lifelong student of the art of managing. In her continuing development she will surely probe the classic and current writing on management.

Management is not a job; it is a profession—a dynamic, challenging, and often creative profession. It has been described quite aptly as the oldest of the arts yet the youngest of the professions. The image of a profession is mirrored by the performance of its most competent practitioners. Hopefully, you are or will be one of these pros—a more professional manager.

NATHANIEL STEWART

Seaford, New York
February 1978

Contents

CHAPTER 3

*The Effective Woman Manager as a Coordinator:
Your Contribution to Company Effectiveness*   **51**

CHAPTER 4

*The Effective Woman Manager as a Delegator:
Managing the Allocation of Priorities, Projects, and
Decisions*   **67**

Contents

CHAPTER 5

*The Effective Woman Manager as an Evaluator in the
Management of Ideas, Advice, Proposals*　　　　**97**

CHAPTER 6

*The Effective Woman Manager as a Problem-Solver
and Decision-Maker*　　　　**121**

Contents   xvii

CHAPTER 8

The Effective Woman Manager as a Trainer and Guide: Developing the Human Resources of Your Staff   **173**

The Effective Woman Manager

CHAPTER ONE

The Effective Woman Manager

AS A PROFESSIONAL MANAGER

NOW THAT YOU'RE HERE

The appearance of a new woman manager on the scene produces neither instant credibility nor instant alarm, but an attitude of "Let's wait and see." More and more, the reaction to a new female manager is one of open-mindedness, receptiveness accompanied by suspended judgment and the desire to give her a chance to show her abilities. This is not unusual, however; employees and colleagues have long known that the selection and designation of managers is highly fallible. Some managers prove to be competent; others are "lemons;" and still others turn out to be marginal and have to be carried through the efforts of others. This applies to all managers, male and female.

During the "wait and see" period, people have unexpressed questions that affect their own well-being and that of the department or the division: Does she really know the role of a manager? Can she demonstrate ability to meet the responsibilities of this job? Will this new environment "throw her," since it is not the conventional setting for a woman? Will she be able to stand on her own, with no more than the usual cooperation extended to a boss by subordinates and associates? They try to judge the extent to which she shows early signs of mastering role, skills, relationships in giving managerial leadership to the particular department or division, branch or plant of the company.

Success stories about the woman manager focus largely on "how to get there"—how a woman can break into supervisory and managerial ranks. In this legitimate preoccupation with a woman's opportunities to break into management, there has been great emphasis on sources, preparedness, and channels of entry to such positions: company traineeships, the master's in business administration, career counseling, assertiveness training, job rotation, the influence of an older mentor in the company who shows the way to the internal reward system, assessment centers for predicting the promotables, and even tokenism as a questionable but practical beginning.

The focus of this chapter is more important: your role as

manager once you get there. It deals with perspectives of the modern manager's job; the managerial role—what the organization expects of the manager in terms of performance; the main elements of managing; and the idea of authority and its proper use. Having "gotten there," you must stay there and measure up to expectations, if you are to move on to positions of greater responsibility.

THE ROLE OF THE MANAGER

The manager, at every level, is deputized to do that which is necessary to enable the company to attain certain goals. The company provides a "road map" in terms of specific goals, expressed policies, operating systems, qualified workers, some essential controls, and physical resources. Within these parameters, with resources and performance standards, the manager is entrusted to make decisions and produce desired results leading toward these goals. In short, the role of manager is to harness and use all resources—people, talent, ideas, time, money, systems, energies, space, technology, computer instruments, information, and so on—in making decisions which contribute to the company's fulfillment of goals.

The role of the professional manager has several aspects: first, basic responsibilities and expectations inherent in the modern manager's job; second, the kind of leadership exercised in meeting these responsibilities and standards of performance; third, the judicious use of authority; and, fourth, the cultivation of an organizational "climate" conducive to willing and continuing productive effort. All aspects mesh in the evaluation of the professional manager. Although other internal and external influences also affect her performance and the way it is judged, as these are fundamental.

There are other interpretations of the managerial role. One of the pioneers in the management movement, Chester Barnard, saw it largely as attaining coordination and cooperation among people. A noted psychologist, Mason Haire, saw organization as a living organism and the role of the manager as one of coping with the problems of adaptation as this organism was affected by the environment. Charles Hughes, of Texas Instruments, sees mutual goal-setting and leading people toward the pursuit of such goals as the main commitment for the manager in today's business and industrial world. Others see organization as a social (communal) concern in which the manager's role is to understand and work with employee values, norms, and group behavior in the work setting. Michael Maccoby presents the manager as gamesman or gameswoman, taking the position that, given our economic system and its stimulation of greed (that is, money as the prime symbol of corporate victory), the image of the gamesman or gameswoman as winning one game after another in the corporate battle is appropriate. Other critics, however, give the nod to competitiveness but deplore the cult of gamesmanship.

THE MANAGER'S JOB—HEIGHTENED EXPECTATIONS

There was a time when two expectations of a good manager dominated: to stay "on top of things" in day-to-day operations, and to produce short-term results. Today these bread-and-butter expectations no longer seem acceptable in themselves. The scope has been broadened, as shown.

The Modern Manager's Job: Expectations

Today, the manager is expected to establish a balance between short-term results and longer-term outlook. The expectations of the manager's job, in attaining this balance, involve her:

Staying on top of things in day-to-day operational management.

Reinforcing working relationships—upward, downward, and laterally with superiors, colleagues, and subordinates.

Being problem-oriented and making effective and timely decisions:

Anticipating problems.

Identifying the real nature of the problems.

Analyzing problems

Developing proposed solutions or options to deal with the problems

Managing toward attainment of

Goals.
Targets.
Priorities.
Objectives.

Consistent with those agreed upon jointly with superiors, colleagues, and subordinates.

Innovating in various ways; through

New approaches

Changes

Experimentation.

Plans for new or enlarged programs.

Mechanization, where feasible and more productive.

Organizational improvement.

Better utilization of people, space, facilities, other resources.

Various contributory activities.

Economies.

Use of newer tools of management.

LEADERSHIP CONTENT—GENERAL SUMMATION

There have been many approaches to the definition of leadership in business. Some compare it with military and political leadership in defining a core of leadership qualities. Others stress the unique qualities of the robber barons, land speculators, and one-product inventors who found a ready market for their products and achieved instant wealth. Monopolists who ran afoul of the regulatory commissions and the courts have been seen as heroic leaders. Both self-made men and women and inheritors of established business empires have been defined as business leaders.

From 1930 through the 1950s, industrial psychologists and management journalists tried to draw profiles of business leaders in terms of key traits. The range of descriptive traits was without limit: drive, initiative, perseverance, imagination, pride, aggressiveness, patience, emotional stability, consistency, decisiveness, loyalty, moral values, inspirational qualities, intuitiveness. This tendency to portray leaders in terms of traits, temperament, and personality characteristics had its field day, but proved to have limited utility, since one could always find leaders who lacked these supposedly defining characteristics.

With the advent of the executive development movement, writers shifted to the identification of leadership "styles." Leaders were classified as bureaucratic, democratic, autocratic, "particratic," free-rein, even quarterback, diplomat, and commander. The autocrat was refined so that exploitive autocrat and benevolent autocrat could be distinguished. More recent classifications include Robert Blake's managerial grid—"9,1" manager, the "5,5" manager, the "9,9" manager, interpreted in terms of their degree of concern for production or for people. Freudians have also tried to interpret the industrialist leader, as have advocates of the T-group and sensitivity training for managers. Recently, a trend has emerged, which highlights these views of business leadership:

1. Leadership is not a matter of who the person is, but of what she does.

2. Leadership is situational. Different jobs require different clusters of leadership assets.

3. Leadership is largely the art of getting things done through people—mobilizing people, technology, information, ideas, funds, and other resources, and using this totality effectively.

4. Leadership is the cultivation of a sound organizational "climate" in which people grow as they contribute to the company's objectives.

5. Leadership is the ability to persuade others to work enthusiastically and competently toward defined objectives.

6. Although personal abilities help determine the quality of leadership, so do the caliber of one's followers, the clarity and worthiness of the goals, and the pressure of the environment;

7. Leadership involves a combination of technical, human, and conceptual skills.

8. Leadership is the art of formulating goals and developing sound strategies and approaches in attaining them.

9. Leadership is the balanced attainment of short-term results and long-term aspirations of the business enterprise.

10. Since leadership is an expression of accomplishment by its

followers, leadership is gauged by how much they understand about the goals pursued, how they perform, how unified they are in the work setting, and how committed they are toward the attainment of goals.

From this a distinction emerges between the *charismatic* and the *professional* leader. Moreover, in viewing and evaluating the professional leader in organization, we must distinguish between executive leadership, middle-management leadership, and supervisory leadership, since all three are vital to organizational effectiveness.

Organizational leadership has been defined as role behavior which unites and stimulates followers to pursue particular objectives in particular environments. The professional leader determines the most appropriate and productive role behavior in dealing with followers, goals, environment, and her own leadership abilities, and must integrate corporate values, group values, and individual values productively to attain the company's goals.

James Cribbin, of the American Management Association, sees leadership on the job as

> a process of interpersonal influence on the activities of an organized group, principally by means of competence, motivation, and communication, with the purpose of goal setting, goal acceptance, and goal achievement.

For those seeking the basic characteristics that distinguish effective and ineffective managers, Dr. Cribben, like many other researchers, holds that there are no "universal" characteristics of effective leaders. But there are valuable assets that a manager may develop more fully. Dr. Cribben stresses, for example:

1. Present performance. Ability to perform duties very well in one's present position.

2. Initiative. Ability to be a "self starter."

3. Acceptance. Ability to gain respect and win the confidence of others.

4. Analysis and judgment. Ability to reach sound conclusions based on evidence.

5. Communication. Ability to "get through" to people at all levels.

6. Accomplishment. Amount and quality of work produced through the effective use of time.

7. Flexibility. Ability to cope with change, to adjust to the unexpected.

8. Objectivity. Ability to control personal feelings; open-mindedness.*

If one were to convert these abilities into action or view the manager behaviorally, she would show a balanced profile rather than a mix of exceptional strengths and weaknesses. Observers see this behavioral profile of the successful manager:

Maintains stability of the organizational unit during periods or situations of stress, adversity, and emergency;

Sets a sound code of ethical conduct, through her own example, for her subordinates.

Knows what really motivates people to higher performance and sets the climate in which the full talents of people can thrive and be fully utilized.

Keeps an eye on major objectives constantly, and tests actions and decisions against this base.

*Adapted from James Cribbin, *Sense and Nonsense About Leadership,* United Hospital Fund, Training, Research, and Special Studies Division, New York, 1967, p. 19. Reprinted by permission of the United Hospital Fund of New York.

Is both effective and open in communicating with others, knowing that candor is generally the basis of credibility and trust in communication.

Plans well for short-term, intermediate, and long-term results.

Accepts the reality that conflict as well as cooperation is part of managerial life and must be confronted and resolved.

Learns the need for and the reasons behind change, has the courage to make or implement changes, is aware of the psychological reactions of those affected by changes, and does all that is required to execute them in the best interests of the enterprise.

Makes fewer mistakes than other managers in deciding when to take risks and when to move conservatively.

Has a realistic grasp of the financial aspects of the organization, shows responsiveness to need for economies and cost control, and is able to draw meaningful implications from accounting data.

Acts promptly and wisely in furthering the image and reputation of the company in any external relationships with contractors, vendors, competitors, and others.

Does not worry unduly about making decisions; makes them rationally and in good time, and studies the outcome or effects; and knows which decision-making problems can be delegated to competent subordinates.

Can tolerate more uncertainty and ambiguity than others in the business environment.

Works effectively in coordinated efforts with other department managers as needed.

MORE ABOUT THE MANAGER

The preceding section only summarizes highlights of the leadership role in business management. Writers and counselors, readers and career-seekers in management all know that the managerial *role* can be treated too broadly and the subject of managerial *assets* and capabilities too lightly. The woman manager is continually developing, and she will find useful guidance in additional reading, especially in the significant writings from the 1950s to the present. Peter Drucker in *The Effective Executive* gives a provocative discussion of managerial practices that help one attain better results and make more effective decisions. *The Professional Manager,* a volume of essays by the late Douglas McGregor, edited by his wife, Caroline McGregor, focuses on the interpersonal behavior of the manager and on problems of power, control, and conflict resolution in the modern organization. Dr. Cribbin's *Effective Managerial Leadership,* already referred to, spans many areas, from the nature of management to problems of business ethics and corporate conduct. David Ewing, in *The Managerial Mind,* focuses on the intellectual characteristics that distinguish the manager's approach to problems from that of people in other fields, yet also deals with the dilemmas of conformity, manipulation, administrative creativity, and organizational pressures. Marvin Bower, the noted economist who helped build McKinsey & Company as a management counsulting firm of international prestige, covers both philosophy and action in his book *The Will to Manage.* The new manager will find F.M. Lopez' *The Making of a Manager* a probing and rewarding work, describing the ways in which managers are selected, developed, and promoted in American business and industry. Drucker's monumental *Management: Tasks, Responsibilities, and Practices* is still an invaluable source for self-education. Stewart's *Strategies of Managing for Results,* based on featured writings in *Nation's Business,* has been regarded as extremely helpful for its focus on practical, day-to-day management in the middle echelons of corporate life. Of the many articles in professional journals, *Skills of an Effective Administrator,* by Robert Katz which appeared originally in the *Harvard Business Review,* is one of the best basic accounts. The field of management abounds in good books and journals for the woman in her continuing self-development as a manager.

AUTHORITY AND ITS USE—CRUCIAL TO THE MANAGERIAL ROLE

There are many casualties among those who misused authority in their eagerness to exercise newly found power. One must understand the nature of authority in order to guard against this hazard. An understanding of authority involves the following: recognition of its source (from whom, to whom, limitations, how derived, where originated); differentiation (not the same as excessiveness, power, personal reward and punishment, abuse); identification (kind of authority, extent or degree, provisions); its tendency to arouse emotions (e.g., domination, fear, distrust, among workers); and its relationship to decision-making (applicability, timing, coordinative effort in teamwork, link to responsibilities).

Authority is the *legitimate* possession and exercise of the right to command others to act in a manner that furthers the purposes and best interests of the enterprise. It is sometimes seen as legitimate power, acceptable to those supervised, as against power linked to the threat of coercion. Indeed, *influence* is often seen as more important and broader than authority, since influence is a behavioral capability—the ability to persuade people to act to promote the fulfillment of policies and goals.

Authority itself has several meanings. It can mean (1) the formal authority conveyed by rank, title, or position to give orders to others; (2) the tendency for subordinates to obey, partially obey, or even ignore the orders of the superior; (3) the authority inherent in the job itself by virtue of its responsibilities; (4) the difference between conferred authority (title) and earned authority. Finally, other concepts—the authority of competence, the authority of ideas, the authority of character, and the authority of precedent and history—are distinguished from the authority of position in and of itself.

Authority is often *limited*. The organization manual, the job description, the management-union contract provisions, delegation, periodic performance review and its consequent revision of authority, special executive orders, and other factors all constrain authority. Moreover, authority can also be *resisted* by subordinates through group inaction, grievances, or informal organization. Subordinates may work through direct confrontation by subtle ways, and, by other means when authority is felt to be unwarranted, excessive, threatening, or abusive. The doctrine of "consent of the governed" is not to be taken lightly in the business organization. Line authority must be differentiated from functional or staff authority. The former deals with chain-of-command relationships and the latter with functional direction—for example, from the purchasing department about order procedures, the personnel department about recruitment commitments, or the quality control unit about technical specifications of components.

The limitations on absolute authority are sometimes formalized in expressions of different *degrees* of authority: pending authority, authority subject to review by . . . , concurrent authority with another department, special authority exercised only as granted, delegated authority granted for a limited duration and for a particular project, and full authority consistent with organizational policies, structure, and working relationships. Final or ultimate authority resides only in the office of the company president or with the board of directors.

The manager should identify the *locale* in which each kind of authority is exercised. In each area—for example, in finance, library resources, standards, facilities, maintenance, relationships with the local press, budgetary revisions, program adjustments, cost control, and personnel reassignments—identify the source of authority and what it means for your decision-making.

Since a statement of authority is associated with a position rather than with an individual incumbent, and is defined in terms of the responsibilities of that position, such authorization is most usefully expressed in terms of verbs of managerial action. It is helpful to "pin down" another's authority, as well as your own, by expressing it specifically. For example, you can distinguish

One's authority to:

Approve/disapprove.	Initiate action.
Requisition.	Organize or reorganize.
Allocate.	Maintain liaison.
Install changes.	Expedite.
Supervise.	Waive or make exceptions.
Schedule or reschedule.	Consult.
Formulate.	Give priority to . . .
Develop.	Recommend.
Investigate.	Experiment.
Contract for . . .	Coordinate with . . .
Evaluate.	Direct.
Assign.	Delegate.
Authorize.	Issue orders.
Review.	Establish rules.
Deputize.	Execute.
Plan.	Implement.
	Exercise control over . . .

Remember that *acceptance* of authority measures by subordinates or the work group is critical to the exercise of authority, and that *earned* authority—respect derived through competence, ideas, contribution, character—is more persuasive than conferred authority.

What are the key problem areas in the exercise of authority? The following are most widely recognized for their one-time or continuing impact upon organizational behavior and the responsiveness of groups and individuals.

Abuse rather than legitimate use of authority.

Lack of clarity about formal, conferred authority and informal, assumed authority.

Overlapping of authority between individuals at different levels or with different functions.

Authority assumed by staff officials which really belongs to those with line responsibility.

Fragmented rather than full authority.

Authority inconsistent with attached responsibilities.

Failure to delegate authority sufficiently.

Authority used as power and overextended in a show of power.

Lack of clarity as to designations—for example, full authority, limited authority, special authority only as granted, authority subject to review by, pending authority, or other qualification of authority.

Reluctance to accept authority, or reluctance to use authority once accepted.

Unwillingness to modify authority in light of a situation;

Inconsistency in the exercise of authority.

Earl Strong, the management educator and author, makes a perceptive distinction between "power over" and "power through" as it relates to the concept of authority. "The manager who wants power over people . . . has confused means with ends," he contends. "The manager needs power *through* people in order to get power *over* results." The professional manager recognizes this point and encourages each subordinate to make the most of his or her abilities, potential, and gain in respect for one's full contribution to goal attainment.

How-to Guidelines for the Manager

Although there are no certainties or formulas for success as a manager, the distillation of extensive experience, research, and other knowledge can help the woman manager meet the demands of the job. Some of these guidelines are presented below in counseling the manager on the broader aspects. Later chapters, dealing with each special skill, offer more specifics, "how-to," guidance.

In the broad context, here are some vital pointers:

Know your own job well—its key responsibilities, its measure of authority, and the standards of performance associated with the job. Know, and even anticipate, your boss's further expectations beyond written performance standards. Be ready to meet them. Make adaptations as the job is changed or modified either directly or organizationally.

Expect to live with risk. There is no such thing as riskless management. There is only the intelligent handling of risk. Good planning, some research, capitalizing on the participation and ideas of your people, and good controls help minimize risk.

Be neither dominant nor dominated. Just be a responsible and a responsive professional manager.

Keep the lines open to your superior; be attuned to the boss's big three "p's"—plans, priorities, and programs—which stem from the overall goals. Know them well and stay on top them.

Keep the lines open to your key employees, so that you always have timely and adequate feedback on progress and problems on the job, whether good news or bad.

Be ready to give assistance, encouragement, and recognition, not just receive it.

Guard against the complacency trap. Learn more about the organization and its workings; grow beyond your present specialization; and, despite the good job this past quarter, determine to do even better this next quarter.

Use your authority as needed in the situation and with discretion, rather than wield it as an instrument of ego and threat.

Formulate, jointly with your employee, standards of performance for each of their jobs, and judge them against these standards, not on vague or unstated criteria.

Be alert to work simplification and method improvement, not merely for budgetary savings but for organizational efficiency and job satisfaction.

Be patient. Some programs will move faster, some employees work faster, some problems are resolved sooner, some results are visible sooner than others. Monitor, overlook the operations of the total department or division, be aware of timetables and deadlines, but exercise patience for the many situations which require it.

Learn to take criticism constructively and without "blowing up," and give criticism the same way.

Learn the ways of bureaucracy in the internal organization, but do not become a bureaucrat yourself.

Be alert to motivational influences which make your people tick. In most cases motivating employees accomplishes more than driving them.

Recognize the vagaries in decision-making: Some aspects of decision-making are challenging and exciting, but there are other kinds which are sheer drudgery and often unpleasant. Nevertheless, you are expected to make *all* decisions which fall within your domain as a manager.

Take on new responsibilities as the opportunities arise; however, do this prudently and cumulatively without impairing your ability to handle the present scope of responsibilities or otherwise risking imbalance in your management of the unit.

Guard against becoming easily upset by minor things at the expense of the more vital and important matters in the daily job.

Be innovative as much as is practicable, and, in doing so, tap the ideas of your people as well as your own. A new plan, an improvement, an experiment, a change, a revised system, a different approach, better utilization—all are evidence of innovative thinking.

Plan in the context of short-term, intermediate, and long-term targets.

Use your managerial time wisely and match time with responsibilities.

Exercise surveillance over your organizational units and check on the caliber of problem-solving and decision-making which goes on at the subordinate levels.

Criticize unproductive effort, marginal performance, and poor results, but do not take over. Stress the quantity and quality factors you expect, and observe carefully how your criticism and expectations are responded to.

Show backbone in dealing with office politics, obsolescence, conflict, blind spots, and other matters which impair organizational effectiveness and working relationships.

Solve problems in such a way and with such depth that they will *stay* solved and do not reappear.

Act, don't react. Don't fall victim to the occupational hazard of putting out fires, handling emergencies, or otherwise managing by crisis situations.

Know the difference between friendships and cronyism. Cultivate and value personal and professional friendships, and avoid the charge of cronyism which may affect your objectivity and decision-making on the job.

Dr. Philip Marvin, consultant to General Foods Corporation and other major firms, offers these guidelines for the professional manager:

Don't be managed by time; be a full-time manager of time.

Don't do it yourself; get it done through others.

Don't stand still; be a (manager) on the move.

Don't make people do things; motivate them to want to do things.

Don't let your people become obsolete; develop in them new capabilities to meet new needs.

Don't hope it happens; define commitments.

Don't try to ride off in all directions; make alignment of aims a total commitment.

Don't let the 'loner' limit his or her output; give the job to team people.

Don't make decisions; develop decision-makers.*

*Adapted from Philip Marvin, *Multiplying Management Effectiveness,* New York, American Management Associations, 1971, p. IX Reprinted with permission of the American Management Associations.

James L. Hayes, president of the American Management Association, stresses that credibility creates trust; thus, it is important for the manager to be fully aware of the significance of making promises and keeping promises once made. For all the emphasis focused on the manager as a problem-solver, Dr. Hayes reminds us that the effective manager is also a problem-preventer.

Self Audit: Are You a Good Manager?

Note: In company programs your superior will generally rate or appraise you on the exercise of important managing skills as shown below.* You can also do it yourself periodically. Try it: rate yourself; enter candid comments about your performance on each skill; state your plans for self-improvement.

Planning Skill—degree to which incumbent:

<u>   (CHECK ONE)   </u>

Assessed and established priorities of result area.
Designed realistic short and long range plans.
Formulated feasible timetables.
Anticipated possible problems and obstacles
reaching required results.

Poorly
Minimally Acceptable
About Average
Quite High
Outstanding

Comments:

Organizing Skill—degree to which incumbent:

<u>   (CHECK ONE)   </u>

Grouped activities for optimal use of personnel and
material resources in order to achieve goals.
Clearly defined responsibilities and authority limits
of subordinates.
Minimized confusion and inefficiencies in
work operations.

Outstanding
Quite High
About Average
Minimally Acceptable
Poorly

Comments:

*Adapted from the management appraisal program and reproduced with permission of Eastern Air Lines, Inc.

Controlling Skill—degree to which incumbent:

                     (CHECK ONE)

                     Poorly

Established appropriate procedures to be kept   Minimally Acceptable
informed of subordinates' work progress.
Identified deviations in work goal progress.   About Average
Adjusted to deviations in work to insure   Quite High
that established goals were met.   Outstanding

Comments:

Problem-Solving Skill—degree to which incumbent:

                     (CHECK ONE)

                     Outstanding

Demonstrated ability to isolate and define   Quite High
problem areas clearly.
Effectively identified and evaluated alternative   About Average
solutions.   Minimally Acceptable
Was able to determine true nature of problem   Poorly
rather than deal with its symptoms.

Comments:

Decision-Making Skill—degree to which incumbent:

                     (CHECK ONE)

                     Poorly

Exercised good judgment in taking appropriate   Minimally Acceptable
action based on all available information.
Recognized decisions that had to be deferred until   About Average
all pertinent facts were gathered and analyzed.   Quite High
Willingly made necessary decisions relating   Outstanding
to work area.
Accepted responsibility for following through
on her own and her subordinate's decisions.

Comments:

Directing Skill—degree to which incumbent:

                     (CHECK ONE)

                     Outstanding

Motivated and influenced subordinates to meet   Quite High
or exceed work goals.
Made effective assignments based upon   About Average
demonstrated skills and knowledge.   Minimally Acceptable
Utilized available organizational resources   Poorly
to accomplish the goals of her unit.

Comments:

Ability to Develop Subordinates—degree to which
incumbent:

    (CHECK ONE)

Poorly _____

Minimally Acceptable _____

About Average _____

Quite High _____

Outstanding _____

    Provided opportunities for subordinates to have a
variety of experiences designed to challenge their
capabilities and develop knowledge and skills
necessary for task and career advancement.
Took appropriate steps to have backups and
replacements groomed for key positions.

Comments:

_____

_____

Interpersonal Skill—degree to which incumbent:

    (CHECK ONE)

Outstanding _____

Quite High _____

About Average _____

Minimally Acceptable _____

Poorly _____

    Demonstrated a genuine concern for the needs and
feelings of others in discharging her responsibilities.
Related well with all levels of personnel.
Encouraged participation, teamwork, and established an open and trusting work environment.

Comments:

_____

_____

Communication Skill—degree to which incumbent:

    (CHECK ONE)

Poorly _____

Minimally Acceptable _____

About Average _____

Quite High _____

Outstanding _____

    Demonstrated sound business writing skills that
enabled her to prepare clear and concise reports
and correspondence.
Demonstrated effective oral presentation skills that
enabled her to get ideas across to superiors,
subordinates, and peers distinctly and convincingly.
Recognized communication breakdowns and took the
necessary corrective action.

Comments:

_____

_____

Industry Knowledge—degree to which incumbent:

    (CHECK ONE)

Outstanding _____

Quite High _____

About Average _____

Minimally Acceptable _____

Poorly _____

    Demonstrated knowledge of industry practices,
regulations, and governmental rules in her
technical area.
Was knowledgeable regarding persons, agencies, and
organizations relevant to her responsibilities.

Comments:

_____

_____

Organizational Knowledge—degree to which incumbent:

Demonstrated familiarity with company goals, essential personnel, policies, procedures, and concerns of the organization.
Utilized such knowledge in the performance of her responsibilities.

(CHECK ONE)
Poorly
Minimally Acceptable
About Average
Quite High
Outstanding

Comments:

Technical Knowledge and Skills—degree to which incumbent:

Demonstrated technical job knowledge and skills essential to the effective performance of current position responsibilities.
Was technically well informed about those jobs over which she has supervisory responsibilities, as well as related positions in her functional area.

(CHECK ONE)
Outstanding
Quite High
About Average
Minimally Acceptable
Poorly

Comments:

CHAPTER TWO

The Effective Woman Manager

AS A PLANNER

Charting Routes to Accomplishment

THE POTENTIAL IS THERE: TAP IT

Countless women have proved themselves highly competent planners in the mainstream of life. Their affinity for planning is good evidence of their potential as planners in management.

Political candidates have successfully campaigned on the road, leaving all their planning activities to competent women in the political organization. In industry, women have planned and ensured the continued smooth functioning of the office during the extended absences of their superiors. Women's involvement has been notable in the planning activities of church, social, philanthropic, and service-related organizations in the community. During physical disasters—floods, hurricanes, epidemics, and other major crises—they have been in the forefront of planning for evacuation, medical assistance, temporary housing, and other general needs. They have traditionally had a primary role in planning for their children's short-term needs and long-term career development. The economics of the home—budgeting, financial outlays, and other use of money assets—is often entrusted to the planning skills of the woman. From early childhood on, women have planned with others in the allocation of work duties on the farm and in the home. Historically, life on the American frontier was as dependent on the woman as on the man for meeting daily exigencies.

What, then, inhibits their capacities as planners in the management setting? Primarily, it is the fact that they have been forced to examine the trees without getting a chance to look at the forest. They have been denied broad boundaries and vistas, vantage points from which to appreciate the complexity of landscape and alternative routes for crossing the terrain. The perspective has been office bound, confined to very specific daily tasks, specific records, specific visitors or clients, specific organizational procedures and regulations, and other limiting features which hamper their outlook as prospective managers.

Another factor hindering the woman's preparedness for managing and planning is the parochialism of the duties of a low-level supervisory position. Traditionally, supervisors have been conduits through which plans are executed rather than planners in their own right. The little planning expected of them is generally limited to the allocation of work, elementary scheduling, coverage for absenteeism, anticipation of the need for reordering or requisitioning raw material, and preparation of production reports. Despite the rhetoric about the importance of the first-line supervisor as a member of the management team and his or her involvement in departmental or divisional affairs, the fact is that such responsibilities are kept at a minimal, pedestrian level. The first-line supervisory position generally does not offer much incentive or opportunity to be linked to operational planning in its broader sense. Consequently, the woman serving as supervisor in a bank, retail store, insurance firm, chemical plant, or other business, and especially in repeating the same duties year after year with little variation in responsibilities, does not grow in ability as a planner.

The third inhibiting factor relates largely to those women who serve in a staff role to other managers—researching, developing information, preparing feasibility studies, making recommendations, yet standing on the sidelines. The contribution they make is primarily toward the germination of a plan, the initial stages of selection and design. In such cases they see only half the sphere, and are denied the opportunity to see the half which involves converting the intellectual plan into *action planning*. Since the latter falls outside of their responsibilities as staff aides, they cannot experience the realities of putting plans into action. While part of that reality is the joy of witnessing plans fulfilled, much is beset with delays, frustrations, obstacles, misunderstandings, and other factors which impede the implementation of plans. To be denied this opportunity is to be deprived of intensive, hard knocks line experience so valuable to the aspiring woman manager.

The fourth obstacle has been the cultural stereotype of the woman assistant who is expected to carry through new procedures or methods without asking questions about their rationale. Subordination fosters submissiveness, and the cultural mores of business management have long sustained the meek compliance of the humble subordinate. The result has been detachment from the arena of thinking and planning.

In short, the potential is there. The investigative studies by the team of Reif, Newstrom, and Monczka demonstrate strongly that women have strong attributes as potential planners—a capacity for abstract reasoning, analytic skills, achievement motivation, and adaptability, and that they are no different from men in this respect. Furthermore, the Jacklin and Maccoby studies clearly establish the conclusion that women have no psychological handicaps that would limit them in planning or other management functions.

SOME MISCONCEPTIONS AND HOW TO CORRECT THEM

A number of misconceptions or myths exist about planning as a management function. Many women are prone to these misconceptions because of their limited experience in management echelons and, perhaps, their awe of planners in the world of business. There exists, for example, the view that somewhere in the corporate heavens some omniscient being can see into the future, make a precise forecast, promptly prepare a master plan, and with a flash of divine authority put it into effect. This view of an executive charged with planning the destiny of the organization, who has a close kinship and personal communion with the Almighty, is a myth. The higher the executive, the more he or she is burdened with the great uncertainties that can spell fortune or doom for the corporation. One struggles with the critical risks to be taken, and is in constant search for "intelligence"—the kind of fresh, verifiable, vital, and quantifiable information on which to base a new plan.

Good planning is disseminated at several levels, among a number of people, and comes only with hard work. It is not the private realm of one person at the apex of the organization (although strategic plans for the company's future are part of executive leadership); it permeates the entire organization. There are grand plans which evolve into broad sector plans, which in turn produce departmental plans, until, ultimately, the lowest-level operational work plans are devised. The principle of pervasiveness of company-wide planning is a dominant one in the modern, progressive organization.

Another common misconception is that a plan emerges full-blown—balanced, well integrated, comprehensive, thorough, ready for presentation with a flourish of drums and trumpets. Again, this is far from the truth. Many plans are imprecise, unworkable as drawn, unimaginative, and developed without having had all the "bugs" removed. It is because of this vulnerability that most planning is *not* a one-time concentrated effort but a *continuing process,* reviewed periodically, defended if need be, its excesses and gaps corrected, and its integrative consequence and results constantly pursued. Wherever there is planning there are planners, and many planners are fallible, narrow in their outlook, timid, biased, prone to procrastinate, starry-eyed, or rigid. Thus, the processes of checks and balances, control and review, disclosure and correction are important to the planning function.

A third misconception is the separation of planning from action. This is a corporate luxury which exists in the relatively few places endowed with a high-salaried planning staff, prestigious planning committees, invited consulting economists, and country retreats for reflective discussions. And there is serious debate as to whether such planning staffs really pay their way. Planning and action are really aspects of a single complex process. One aspect demands your alertness, insights, intellectual probing, and creativeness in generating a plan, a design. The other calls upon your experience, sense of realism, understanding of systems and procedures, persuasiveness, knowledge of people in the work environment, and special skills in shaping the plan into a form that can be put into practice. Thus, most managers have to be both planners and doers, in the sense that comprehensive and effective planning is the outcome of both intellectualism and artisanship, the conceptual and the operational. Weakness in one *or* the other can damage the entire planning effort.

A fourth misconception is the "they can't mean me" syndrome. There is a tendency on the part of relatively inexperienced managers to feel that they should be in on the planning effort, yet they remain nonparticipants. The reasons for this may vary. Perhaps they are outranked or outflanked, and their views don't get a hearing. Or they may prefer to be encumbered at their desks with day-to-day tasks and the security of discharging routine responsibilities rather than taking on the more complex task of planning, with its controversy and risk of failure. It may be that they lack self-confidence. Some may also contend that the planning is outside their functional area: "It's not my territory." The last misconception is especially injurious, for involvement in planning is no different from involvement in any other kind of decision-making. The participation of all parties to the plan is vital, whether it is direct or indirect. The ambivalence that comes with the misconception that "they can't mean me" cannot be sustained very long. Sooner or later the manager must exercise the right to participate in the planning effort.

Finally, there is the misconception that your boss will do the planning for you. (Indeed, many bosses do, and they seize this prerogative away from you. It is an abuse of authority.) Most have their own work load and pressures to contend with, and they expect a subordinate manager to do all the planning for her department or unit. This expectation is built into the performance standards for the manager. Your boss will often be ready to review and discuss the plans that you have formulated, but he or she will not relieve you of your basic responsibility to plan for your unit. This is what differentiates a manager from a technician.

THE SCOPE AND PROCESS OF PLANNING

Planning means looking intently at stated goals and proceeding to develop the blueprint required to achieve them. However laudable the goals may be, nothing moves until plans are developed to make things happen. As an executive of the Celanese Corporation expressed it some years ago: A projection is an educated guess at what may happen; a plan is a design for a specific course of action to make sure that the right thing does happen.

There is a whole universe of planning, so to speak. In terms of scope, there are a number of major areas: financial planning, production planning, market planning, facilities planning, program planning, research and development planning, personnel planning, organizational planning, plant and equipment planning, and other major sectors. Associated with these are the temporal dimensions of planning: short-term, intermediate, and long-range.

A distinction is also made between *strategic* plans and *tactical* or *operational* plans. The former are developed to deal with broad concerns about the *future* of the business: its potential and thrust, new specializations, competition, developing markets, economic forecasts and other long-trend projections, technological advances, payoff from research laboratories, diversification, the corporate image, social responsibility, the principal products and how they may be modified or displaced, mergers and acquisitions, and even the changing nature of the business. Strategic plans deal with the business environment and how it is influenced by population trends, government policies and regulations, the growth of unionism, price structures, national income, political stability, international developments, and other influences. They are developed in an arena of knowns and unknowns, volatile changes, long lead time, large investments, and great risks. They fall within the province of top management.

Tactical or operational planning is focused on making the *present* business more effective: making its administrative organization more efficient, its products and services better, its financial controls more precise, its distribution system more streamlined, its people more productive, its sales penetration more extensive, and its return on investment greater. Operational planning is closely tied to (1) goals—the ends, results, or targets to be attained, and (2) policies—the general credo or set of understandings established by the company to guide the thinking of managers in their decision-making.

Budgets and programs are expressions of plans. A number of companies distinguish several types of planning: *work planning,* which covers recurring work load activities; *project planning,* directed toward special, new, or unique activities; and *improvement planning,* which is concerned with very selective areas where timely or significant improvements may be made and which warrant a fairly high priority. Within the parameter of work plans, moreover, one finds single-use plans and standing or repeated-use plans. What are the time dimensions of company planning? They may vary from a week (as in the case of planning for the use of summer interns who are soon to report for work) to a decade (as in the major plans of Xerox, IBM, or ITT). Arbitrarily, short-term planning is conceived within the context of a quarter to a half year; intermediate planning takes place within a time frame of a year to about three years; and long-range planning generally has a range of five years or more.

Obviously, the type of planning undertaken depends on the functional area involved. Some aspects of personnel planning, such as achieving better techniques for testing and interviewing applicants, may warrant a planning time span of one month. In contrast, setting a plan for a research division of a pharmaceutical company in developing a new drug may require a time frame of a year. The pressures for planning may be external, such as the governmental requirement for more safety features to protect the driver of an automobile. Or the pressure may be internal: for example, the need to liquidate or consolidate several units when the means of production are to be changed from manual operations to automated devices.

Companies differ organizationally in the way they undertake

planning. Some use staff specialists for the most part. Others rely largely on committees. Most companies encourage joint participation of line and staff managers in the planning effort. The most universal, and probably the most effective, means is decentralization, or the delegation of major planning responsibility to the operating managers concerned, leaving to their initiative the matter of how best to proceed with the task of planning. However, whatever organizational approach is used, the planning *must* have the support of upper management, and it must be orderly, resourceful, definite, and clearly communicated at essential points of contact.

HOW TO PREPARE A PLAN

One of the essentials in planning is the positing of certain assumptions, conditions, or premises. The premises may be these, for example: the senior citizens market for this product will be saturated and closed within five years; there is a real possibility of improving the quality of this product, without additional cost to the consumer; the tight money situation affecting bank loans to business will ease by June of next year; the availability of chemical engineers will be greater and recruitment will be easier; this function can safely be "farmed out" to a subcontractor without anticipating resistance from the union; twice the present space will be available for us in the new building.

Obviously, the validity of these or other premises can be crucial to the effectiveness of the plan. It is often upon these assumptions that various courses of action are projected and one course of action chosen. The success of planning depends on these assumptions about various conditions. It is important to recognize, therefore, that some conditions are uncontrollable, such as a pending outbreak of war, emergency legislation, a decline in the availability of raw material, or population shifts to the "sun belt" states. Some are, perhaps, semicontrollable: pricing of the product, reduction in labor turnover, attaining a certain share of the market, strengthening management's prerogatives in the next collective bargaining contract, or some other factor. A good number of conditions are controllable. These include, such matters as site selection for a new structure, increased staffing, greater financial support of a research program, expansion at a given rate of 5 percent a year, replacement of obsolescent equipment, improved security measures, greater utilization of the computer facilities, the establishment of new technical specializations, and other conditions that serve as assumptions in planning. Coordinated planning often results in a better and more conscious screening of the premises upon which planning is based, and in a more rational meshing of these different categories of premises. At the level of operational planning, the middle manager's province, most of these factors are controllable. Consequently, her capability in coordinating, communicating, and negotiating with other managers is vital in getting commitment and cooperation on the new plan as it is developed.

The steps in the formulation of a plan are similar to those described in the discussions of decision-making and problem- solving. In planning, however, there is a need for greater awareness of opportunity, for a more binding commitment on the part of the company to "put up" the resources needed to execute the plan, and for constant monitoring to ensure that the "bugs" are removed and revisions made as necessary. Monitoring or control must be regular and precise.

1. The prerequisite to planning, of course, is clarity about the objective or goal in mind. If that goal has already been officially expressed, then attune your planning to it. Should you find that there is no pertinent statement of goal, get it established. Whatever it may be—to reduce absenteeism by 15 percent, to attain a better balance of stock inventories, to regain at least 20 percent of good customers lost to other competitors within the past two years, to improve the records management in the office, to resolve customer complaints within 48 hours, to eliminate the need for overtime pay, to have all documents

ready at least one month before contract renewal time, to further the management development of newly assigned district sales managers, or any other goal—whatever it may be, draft it, get the necessary approval (if needed), codify it in a clear written statement, and communicate it to all concerned.

2. Do the required research. Gather all the pertinent data, records, facts, observations, reports, and other information.

3. Analyze the information and distill the main findings.

4. Establish those assumptions or premises that appear reasonable. To the extent that validation can verify the assumptions, do so.

5. Think through alternate plans and assess their strong and weak points, advantages and disadvantages.

6. Choose the plan that you believe is most promising. Review the important elements of timing, specification, built-in control points, and resources to be allocated to put the plan into effect.

7. Prepare for the action phase by communicating with other managers whose departments may be affected or who may be involved in the execution of the plan. Meet with your subordinates, who have participated in the discussions and formulation of the plan, and now spell out specifically who will be responsible for what, where, and when. Workers should also be informed of the feedback system and the controls provided to check periodically on the execution of the plan and on its results.

WHAT MAKES A PLAN GOOD?

The two main tests of a good plan are these, of course: the extent to which it advances steps toward the attainment of the goal or objective; and the degree to which the gains derived from the plan outweigh the time, money, effort, and other resources spent in preparing and executing it.

But there are other indicators or characteristics of a good plan which become evident throughout the planning process. Among the characteristics of good planning are the following:

Accuracy in "sizing up" the present system or operation.

Perceptiveness in seeing a new opportunity and capitalizing on it.

Extent and quality of research in assembling and consolidating information, data, and other "intelligence."

Anticipation of obstacles to the plan, and reasoning out their effective removal.

Compatibility with other current goals and plans.

Realism in determining additional resources needed.

Caliber of communication (dialogue, presentation, negotiation, coordination, etc.) with comanagers.

Extent of involvement and participation of subordinates in confirming the need for the plan and in providing ideas and proposals.

Feasibility and timeliness.

Discipline in carrying out the plan.

Selection of appropriate controls for feedback of results.

Objectivity of the planner, especially open-mindedness to alternative plans.

Degree of management acceptance and support of the plan.

Edward J. Green, a nationally recognized consultant on the dynamics of planning, points to other characteristics as well. The plan should be reasonably simple and clear so that it can be understood by subordinates, who must integrate it into their own day-to-day activities. It should be adaptable and thus responsive to the various situations in which it will be applied. Flexibility is still another important characteristic. If there are parts of the plan which prove to be unworkable or become obsolete, the plan should be flexible enough to undergo modification, change, or revision as needed. A rigid plan can prove to be a disaster, functionally and psychologically, among the workers.

Most plans, as they are translated into action, require the establishment of priorities and the development of a schedule. This, too, is part of the discipline of planning. Any work plan features some kind of scheduling. Dates for launching the plan, beginning the sequence of actions, reports of progress, and other requirements are important to the entire venture. Among the skills required of a manager, therefore, is the ability to develop meaningful and workable schedules. Sometimes several schedules must be synchronized, especially in the technical and production operations.

LIMITATIONS AND PITFALLS

Despite the opportunity that planning affords for originality, resourcefulness, and initiative, limitations affect the ability to plan well. Unreliability of the forecast, for example, can set in motion a number of difficulties which hinder the planner. Lack of interest or cooperation on the part of the management team will delay the planning effort. A lukewarm attitude on the part of upper management will surely be sensed, and will weaken the planning effort. Lack of representative standardized operations is another inhibiting factor, since it makes quantitative measurement or the application of controls difficult. The total expense of planning—the time, energy, and money expenditure—tends to discourage planning. Periods of very rapid change and the resultant work pressures preclude the opportunity to set aside periods to plan reflectively. The lack of essential records, data, statistics, or evidence of past experiences with the particular operation can be a serious obstacle to intelligent planning. The effort to assemble a plan or report without such essential information is sometimes called "the mathematics of ignorance." Limited available alternatives reduce the prospect of sound planning. Internal conflict among departments presents another serious impediment, since it imposes a severe difficulty in communication, coordination, and cooperation.

Inadequacies, pitfalls, and failures beset the planning function as they do other functions. Setting goals too high or too optimistically can be self-defeating. Failure to anticipate line resistance can spell doom for many a well-reasoned plan. It requires sustained effort and persuasiveness to get policies altered to accommodate the plans—yet if policies are not modified, they obviously will be in conflict with the plan. If the inconsistencies are unresolved or left in limbo, the policy will prevail and the plan will have to be shelved. Conservatism and smugness within the organization can be a potent obstacle. If the planner restricts her sights to her own specialization—the tunnel-vision trap—her limitations will be easily spotted and the plan will likely be rebuffed by others in different specialty areas. Relying on the outside consultant, especially the "expert" who noses around and makes a rapid exit, is another obvious pitfall in serious planning. Excessive fact-finding does not add to the planning effort but only delays it. An organizational climate in which there is an unwillingness to consult or confer clearly impedes planning. One of the more familiar difficulties is the unwillingness to sacrifice short-term disruption for long-term gains. This is a frequent stumbling block.

A healthy philosophy about change and improvement and a healthy attitude of collaboration and good will strongly reinforce the planning effort. Where these are lacking, the most rational plan will be aborted. Lack of competence in the technical areas concerned, poor supervision, and inept handling of people are additional pitfalls to effective planning.

These obstacles are cited not as deterrents to planning, but as "red flags," in order to alert the manager to factors which can defeat the entire investment in the planning effort. The point is that planning cannot be left to chance. The structure and process of planning itself must be sound to counteract or sidestep these obstacles.

LINKAGE TO OBJECTIVES AND POLICIES

Any discussion of planning would be hollow indeed if it did not relate planning to the two closely allied essentials: objectives and policies. Volumes of business literature are devoted to these alone, and the woman manager should continue her self-education by reading in the areas of management by objectives (MBO), policy-formulation, and business decisions.

Although broader objectives are set at the corporate and divisional levels, the middle manager is expected to have her own departmental objectives. In answer to the question "Why departmental objectives?" some of the cogent reasons are listed in the accompanying outline.

Why Departmental Objectives?

To follow through effectively and consistently on corporate or institutional objectives, integrating departmental and corporate objectives.

To provide a better sense of purpose, direction, and total contribution of the department as an organizational unit.

To sharpen goals, timetables, options, and commitments to the attainment of larger objectives.

To enable the department to focus on priorities and payoff matters, and prevent "flying off" on lesser tangents.

To provide more justification for program and budgetary support.

To permit coordination with other units, both early and in later stages, in promoting interdepartmental efforts to attain objectives.

To have a substantial base against which performance or contribution at the department level can be better measured and judged.

To permit more rigorous reexamination of the caliber of planning and control within the department.

To permit development of better performance standards for key subordinates in their "results areas."

Departmental goals must also be realistic, meaningful, attainable, measurable, and communicable. Thus the partnership of manager and subordinates is vital in the formulation and setting of objectives.

Policies are statements of intent and guides to managers in their thinking and decision-making. They serve as the general road map to the destination, the larger objective. Whether her responsibilities as a manager are in purchasing, sales, production, finance, or other function, the woman manager is expected to formulate those policies which are germane to her functional area. There are many advantages in having well-formulated, well-expressed policies for the department. For the management level, it promotes continuity and consistency of decisions, assists in coordination, serves as a good guide to needed control, and provides for a well-disciplined organization. To a considerable extent, it does the same for lower supervision and, in addition, often serves to define jobs and delineate areas of action more explicitly. And, for the workers, the existence of policies tends to assure fairer treatment, helps them see the "big picture," and shows company alertness to the incorporation of new policies and revision of old policies which affect rank and file employees. At times it also serves as an expression of good faith in sharing with the employees matters of mutual concern—safety, job security, nondiscrimination in employment practices, continued training for advancement, the compensation system, and other interests.

As statements of intent and guidelines to decision-making, policies should reflect the philosophy or beliefs of the organization, stated in broad terms, and approved by higher management. They should also have the features of flexibility, acceptability, and clarity for communication and understanding. It is most important to recognize that written policies determine and govern all of the *practices,* procedures, and courses of action to be followed in that particular organizational function. Unless they are amended, existing policies continue to govern.

What makes a "good" policy? Various efforts have been made to define it. Some of the more significant characteristics are these:

It emerges from proved, profitable experiences.

It is generally applicable and can be applied to most situations while allowing for an occasional justifiable exception.

It is written, clear, well understood at all levels, and readily available to those who need to refer to it.

It is consistent with other existing policies and fits well into the various levels of the organization.

It grows out of participation by those affected by it and who have had a hand in its formulation.

It conforms to legal and other mandatory requirements.

It has enough flexibility in interpretation to allow some latitude for discretion by managers in its legitimate application.

It is stable enough to permit effective relationships among managers as well as to promote loyalty and efficiency in implementing it.

It permits the initiation of requests for revision at any time by any level of management affected.

It is periodically subject to review and is responsive to changing circumstances through revision as needed.

The middle manager will find that the task of drafting or writing a policy statement is not an easy one. There is an artfulness about it which comes with experience and with "checking it out" with others. The above characteristics, however, serve as valuable cues to policies and policy-making.

How-to Guidelines for the Planner

Seasoned experience comes only with considerable time. However, some lessons, guidelines, and "pointers" for the woman manager, gained from the distilled experiences of others, should be helpful to her in dealing with this aspect of management. These are presented below.

Anticipate the need for serious planning in some area of operation which is periodically in trouble and needs to be "bailed out." Mull over a possible plan which will be better than an *ad hoc* solution or at best offers only trouble-shooting relief. This kind of incubation is good before sitting down to the task of formally designing a plan.

Bear in mind that, as a planner, you have to be not only logical and rational but also persuasive. You may have to convince your boss, the controller, the head of another department, or even your own subordinates.

Schedules, timetables, and deadlines are important components in many a plan. Set them for yourself, expect your people to set their own once the broad guidelines have been agreed to, and see to it that both you and they respect the target dates.

First things come first. The good planner is perceptive in sensing the real priorities.

Value your time. It is folly to expend major time on minor items. As a planner, you will need time to reflect, probe, research, analyze, confer, design, negotiate, and gain acceptance. This requires considerable "investment time." Make the time you need to plan effectively.

You had better become well versed in the various functions of the company, and the earlier the better. Many plans have a chain-reaction effect on other offices and departments, and the more you are informed about their functions the better the prospect for coordinating and negotiating productively.

Wherever possible, work out plans jointly. This partnership will generate increased understanding and acceptance of your proposal and plan, and if it should ultimately prove to be a good plan with fruitful results, there will be enough credit to go around for all partners.

Be results-conscious rather than routine-minded. The former will ignite the spark for sensing the need for a plan for attaining better results (efficiency, effectiveness, profit, better services, etc.); the latter will keep you deskbound, massaging paper. There are always routine items to be handled, of course, and most of them can better be handled by a subordinate.

An inquiring mind is a valuable asset to the organization. Plans usually spring from the inquiring mind which asks: "I wonder why?" . . . "Might there be a better way?" . . . "Are they aware that we're just spinning wheels?" . . . Don't worry about people who may interpret an inquiring mind as a "nosey" one. Your bosses and peers know the difference between the two.

The well-disciplined planner sets a model for her subordinates. To the extent that they, in turn, become self-sufficient and competent planners at their working level, consider this a major gain for the department.

As a planner, you are engaged in decision-making. Planning is, indeed, a form of decision-making on reaching and revising agreements about what needs to be done, why, when, and how.

It is naive to expect a good plan to evolve and mature by itself. Things do not just happen. Be prepared to allocate a substantial part of your time and energy to it. (And if, occasionally, there is the gift of a flash of insight without much hard work, just consider it a bonus.)

Planning requires an integrative ability: the ability to integrate people with systems, plan with policies and goals, mesh one department's function with that of another, consider both short-term and long-term considerations, and integrate past events, present performance, and future probabilities. It is a formidable ability, to be sure, but it can be built cumulatively and attained.

Your subordinates will inevitably have to be involved in your plans. They have more than technical skills—they have minds. Encourage their participation, tap their minds. When they have had a part in the germination and drafting of the plan, they are more committed to see the plan work successfully.

Make good use of records, data, reports, forecasts, and other "intelligence." They may well fortify your assumptions or premises. Research is part of the job of planning well. The information is generally there. Search it out. However, avoid the trap of excessive fact-finding. The essential and critical information will do. It is not always necessary to have all the information for you to proceed.

Seek help, if you need it. It does not diminish your standing as a manager. The pooling of several minds often pays off better than playing the "loner."

Timing the presentation of a proposal or a plan is vital. Be intuitive enough to sense when it is premature, too late, or about the right moment. Look for cues, signs, moods, and even indiscreet "leaks" of information. Sociability helps, too, in getting some cues on timing.

If you find that your manager is eager to perform radical surgery on your plan, don't feel crushed. (Especially if you and your subordinates, and others with whom you have checked, think well of the plan.) His or her impulse toward surgery probably has little to do with the substance of your plans. It is more likely that other things are troubling your superior, that the pressure is on, or that his or her own ideas have been shot down that very day. Try it again, modifying it slightly in its presentation. Or use alternative plan "B," which is quite good, too.

Do not, above all, *do not* be sneaky. Do not try to push through a plan or get approval in your manager's absence, when you know that he or she has a particular interest or a personal stake in reviewing the plan rigorously and in giving it personal approval. You will generally pay a high price for what is regarded as unethical behavior. (Moreover, even if it should be approved in your manager's absence, it can still be undone or sabotoged.)

There is a place for experimentation. If you and your key subordinates are not fully convinced that the plan is ready for full, official implementation, consider using it for an adequate period on an experimental basis. Then review the results attained and make your final decision accordingly.

Know your own job and know it well—particularly your responsibilities and the boundaries of your authority. You will most likely encounter rough opposition if you develop and present a plan which rightfully comes within the domain of another manager. If you think it falls in some kind of "no man's land" because of the fuzzy allocation of authority, then confer with your own boss or with the other manager about it first.

There are generally some unknowns or unpredictables which can upset the plan when put into practice. Your best insurance against this hazard is to put the emphasis on the *knowns*—the measurable factors, past records, proved judgments, written testimony, evidence of similar plans and results attained elsewhere, and other reasonable knowns.

Have the courage to be critical of a present or a pending plan— its inadequacies, its unfounded assumptions, its unrealistic targets, or its inconsistencies. You would do well to voice your criticism, with some statesmanship. But have the backbone to speak your mind, if it is your conviction that it would be difficult to live with that plan. However, there is a point at which moral courage ends. And if the consensus goes in behalf of the plan and you are outvoted, then you are expected to be loyal to the decision reached by your superior.

Plan to plan. Do not "elbow" this aspect off your agenda.

Flexibility and adaptability are clearly valuable assets of a good planner. They reflect responsiveness to reality and the ability to deal with changing circumstances as they affect the company. They are *not* indicators of "softness," as some people contend. The manager who lets rigidity and bull-headedness take over in an effort to display authority and impose his or her plan through coercion is engaged, in the long run, in a self-defeating exercise.

The elements of scientific method are respected by planners— cause and effect, hypotheses, assumptions, sequence, logic, experimentation, substantive evidence. Be prepared to join the clan. These elements are not incompatible with imagination, creativity, or boldness. They reinforce creativity and bolster bold assertions in sound and acceptable planning.

There is no passing the buck. The planning responsibility is built into the description of every manager's job.

Finally, be prepared to deal in batting averages. Some of your plans will sail through with flying colors; others will be diplomatically shelved for future consideration; and still others will be demolished, rightly or wrongly. Learn to live with adversity. Do not brood. Be resilient and bounce back to hard, productive effort. If you are batting reasonably well, consider yourself a competent planner.

Follow-Up Project: Try Your Hand at Drafting a Plan

Select any two (2) of the situations listed below, which call for the development of a plan.

1. Do as realistic and comprehensive a job as you can in developing a plan. Make your own assumptions, in order to set the stage for the planning exercise.

2. When it has been completed, have someone read and comment on it candidly—perhaps one of your associates, a friend, your boss, or some other individual.

3. Next, make some notes to yourself on the strong points in your behalf in this planning skill and some of the weaker points you may improve in the future.

___

Develop a full plan for any two of the following:

The establishment of a company library, since a number of professional and technical personnel have felt the need for it for some time.

A project to realign and balance out work loads and staffing where there is now some inequity, and complaints are increasing about it.

A transition from the company's present 100 percent military products to a "mix" of 50 percent military products and 50 percent consumer products and services in several new fields.

A customer relations program to improve the quality and promptness of response in dealing with customers or clients.

A plan for active company involvement in community affairs, through which it can develop a better corporate image within the community.

Reduction of excessive long-distance telephone costs in the department.

A physical move of your department to an adjoining building, since the department has been informed that it will have to vacate its present quarters to make room for a large computer center.

An advertising campaign to promote sales volume.

An administrative manual for the department.

A program to attract and recruit professional, subprofessional, technical, and clerical personnel, since the size of your department is to be doubled from its present 21 people to 40 people because of the very rapid growth of the company and most of its departments.

A cost reduction effort to curtail by 10 percent all overhead, production, and other costs because of "belt tightening" in the company—such reductions to reach the target within six months.

Training of supervisors to become more competent in dealing with complaints and grievances.

An official presentation before a consumer protection board in a case where your products have been alleged defective and potentially dangerous to the consumer.

A field trip visit to several branches of your company which have consistently failed to submit reports on time to headquarters.

The launching of a new product (describe its potential, development, testing, manufacturing, up to the point of marketing).

Improvement of the caliber of staff meetings, since there is a prevailing feeling that most of the meetings are dull and unproductive as well as too time-consuming.

CHAPTER THREE

The Effective Woman Manager

AS A COORDINATOR

Your Contribution to
Company Effectiveness

WHAT THEY ARE SAYING

To meet the requirement of directing your own unit, office, or department is an accomplishment, to be sure, but that is only *part* of the manager's job. Since there is a need for unified, integrated action in all types of business enterprise, the manager is also expected to work with comanagers of other units on matters which cut across departmental lines and thus affect all managers jointly. This is a significant aspect of the managerial role, and it puts to the test your willingness and ability to contribute fully to overall company effectiveness. In short, coordination is concerned with well-unified and integrated action directed toward the common goal of the larger organization. Its focus is on joint collaborative effort rather than separatism, and this emphasis often permeates all aspects of company management. To paraphrase John Donne, no woman is an island unto herself.

Reading the "women in management" literature leaves one with these directives on developing the administrative capacity of woman:

See that she gets a broader outlook on the company, and on its goals, functions, and operations.

Take her a step or two beyond her functional specialization and expose her to different ideas, new technologies, varied views.

Help strengthen her building of peer relationships.

Give her more "seasoning" as a manager faced with problems.

Find her some breakthrough into significant experiences related to middle-management responsibilities.

Alert her to the distance or gap which exists between departments and even between boss and subordinate on some matters.

Enable her to make contributions well beyond the ordinary, day-to-day operational activities which cross her desk.

Surely, the opportunity for involvement in the process of coordination and in coordinated activities provides most of the experiences called for in these injunctions. The opportunities should be ample in the course of one's service as a manager.

A RICH OPPORTUNITY FOR UPGRADING

A sure way to establish early visibility among peers, as well as a good measure of credibility as a manager, is to show one's abilities in the art of coordination. The opportunities to do so are abundant. Skill in coordination is a vital part of growth, both the manager's own growth and the company's growth. More and more organizations find it necessary to use such means as task force assignment, committee action, interdisciplinary attack, project management, the matrix structure so popular in the aerospace industry, and other team approaches in order to attain the best results. It is good business and sound management for companies to do so in an era of accelerated change, complexity, internationalism, severe competition, and high risk. Coordination is an effective way to overcome the strains of multiple specializations, to harness the inputs of a number of competent people, to resolve differences on a timely basis, and to integrate the classic management functions with the new and more sophisticated systems in modern organization.

Communication skills are tapped to the utmost in any good coordination venture. Experience has shown that many women managers do have the asset of communicativeness, as well as communication skills. Coordination is an aspect of management which enables them to put these assets to full use. Apart from formal communication channels, such as meetings and progress reports, effective coordination is often reinforced by good *informal* communication. The brief chat, "checking things out" with other managers in drop-in visits, good productive dialogue, the casual but informative memo, the luncheon conversation, the valuable friendship—all of these informal means of communication ease the tasks of achieving better timing, consistency, and understanding as the coordinative venture moves along. The essence of good coordination is balance, collaboration, integration, compatibility. And effective communication has much to do with achieving these goals.

Other advantages are found in coordination. It provides a climate of consultative management, one which requires the woman's full professional contribution. Her ideas and viewpoints are sought out and respected, even if at times not fully accepted, or shelved.

Specialized accomplishment in her own discipline has also been, for the woman, a point of entry to executive office via the side door. It should and can be tapped for more than that, so that ultimate promotion can be direct. In their account of women in management, Loring and Wells advocate career ladders with both lateral and vertical progression. They contend that these paths of mobility must be developed in order to provide ways for women to move out of the traditional pattern of dominating the lower job categories. Involvement in coordinated efforts helps qualify the woman for such movement into echelons beyond the base job categories.

Some observers of the management scene maintain that the task force arrangement makes it easier to accept the leadership of women who might otherwise be resented as bosses in the classic sense of the word. Jane Kay, of the Detroit Edison Company, affirms the view that "a new kind of leadership will be required and that a leader will function as a coordinator rather than that as the authority figure or as a boss."

KNOW COORDINATION APPROACHES AND PATTERNS

Be prepared to fit into any one of several existing coordination patterns. A broad overview of types coordination patterns can serve as a good basis for preparation. First, there is *internal* coordination, concerned with the integration of ideas, plans, functions, and activities within the organization. It is manifested in the coordination of projects in the research and development division, the launching of a major advertising and sales campaign, the conversion to automated systems in production, the effort to reduce safety and health hazards and meet OSHA compliance standards, and the effort to diversify and acquire new products.

Within the broad framework of coordination, it can take on a *vertical* dimension and thus involve either superior-subordinate collaboration or successive levels in the management chain of command. It can also take the shape of *horizontal* coordination. This is more difficult because of the competing interests and specializations of a number of functional units at more or less the same level. An example of the latter is a major insurance company integrating the key people and functions of the underwriting, claims, actuarial, legal, service, finance, and public relations departments. Horizontal coordination can also be seen in an industrial research and development division engaged in projects requiring interdisciplinary understanding and collaborative proposals to solve problems involving the product under investigation, and in which the branches of physics, engineering, chemistry, and metallurgy have comparable organizational status. More frequently, however, horizontal coordination is likely to involve fewer units. Typically, it involves coordination between purchasing and manufacturing, between production and personnel, between engineering and quality control, between sales and finance, or among manufacturing, engineering, and sales. Organizations in fast-paced industries like aircraft, chemicals, office equipment, and electronics find frequent coordination essential to the management of the enterprise.

There is also a pattern of *external* coordination in which the company's managers face needs and problems pertaining to individuals and agencies outside the organization: for example, suppliers, contractors, customers, the press, regulatory agencies, the local community, unions, and others. This type of coordination often involves questions of commitments, clearances and approvals, precedent, cost control, scheduling, policies, and help from others inside and outside the organization.

There are other classifications of coordination. We often refer to "corrective" coordination, designed to rectify an error, correct a dysfunction in the system, eliminate backlogs of reports, or assure availability of equipment and supplies where incidents of nonavailability have caused the loss of time and money. There is "promotive" coordination, based on the premise that there is always a way to improve some operation—make it better, easier, safer, or more economical, and that it takes a team approach to explore and discover improvements. "Preventive" coordination anticipates problems that might occur and devises early action to ward off a possible malfunction or difficulty. It may, for example, anticipate and avert an excessive work load, a flurry of customer complaints, or a series of possible employee grievances. Sometimes there is an overlap of "preventive" and "promotive" coordination. Finally, there is the concept of "programmed" coordination, the kind of coordination that is especially relevant to planning, and in which there is coordination at certain stages, sequences, steps, and other critical periods, at which points managers meet and deliberate on a scheduled basis.

In all respects, the *goal* of coordination, regardless of the type used, is to unify or harmonize policies, plans, programs, and priorities. This balance is attained only as managers acquit themselves well as coordinators or as agents within the coordinative effort.

SOME PITFALLS

There are pitfalls, difficulties, and limitations in coordination, just as in all phases of management. Coordination can be carried to excess. Overcoordination may weaken organizational units, or it may create new, even more acute, problems. In companies that are "coordination happy," few moves can be made, decisions effected, or actions generated before a matter has been cleared with an army of coordinators.

Conflicting or fuzzy goals impose another serious limitation on the manager's ability to carry through her responsibilities as a coordinator or liaison person. Ambiguity about program implementation can be a barrier. The behavior of subordinates is often unpredictable and may impair team effort. Lack of administrative skill in securing agreement and acceptance limits your ability to achieve the degree of coordination you want. Poor organization, and lack of clearly delineated responsibility and authority of officers, may also impede effective coordination.

Other pitfalls range from preoccupation with crash projects, meeting constant emergencies, and handling recurrent troubleshooting ventures, to simply choosing the wrong people for committee or task force work. One easily becomes distressed and prone to "throw in the towel" because of these factors. Yet the manager must be able to contend with the total situation.

Mary Parker Follett, a pioneer in management who advanced the concept of integration and coordination as vital to all organizational accomplishment, was alert to such pitfalls. Her writings acknowledge the constant presence of uncertainty and conflict, yet they stress that in attaining corporate goals, coordination *must* be achieved despite these pitfalls, obstacles, and conflicts.

Toward the solution of this very problem, she proposed certain basic guidelines for management:

Coordinate in the *early* stages, before things reach a state of imbalance that results in dilution of talent, time, energy, and resources.

Coordinate, whenever possible, by direct contact—by face-to-face communication for, exchange of viewpoints, consultation, and effort at reaching understanding and agreement.

Keep in mind the relationship of *all* features of the situation as you coordinate.

Make coordination a *continuing* process.

Good managers know that even the best system has its share of imperfections, and are constantly aware of such weaknesses and of the need to refine, improve, and strengthen the total work effort. Integration *is* management. To these four fundamentals we must now add a fifth of more recent origin: the importance of *consultative* management and participation, gained from many psychological studies of people at work in the modern organization.

JUDGING SUCCESS IN COORDINATION

The concept of "sharedness" is inherent in effective managerial coordination of teamwork, and the heart of "sharedness" is interaction or interpersonal relations. Involved in successful teamwork are five essentials: (1) the extent to which people from different departments and different jobs agree on matters of concern to the company; (2) the degree to which they perceive each other's viewpoints in their work relationships; (3) the extent to which members understand and appreciate the needs and problems of those representing other departments; (4) the degree of willingness to help each other when needed; and (5) the desire and ability to see problems more clearly and cooperate in solving them for the common good and the economic well-being of the company.

Other tests of successful coordination are those which give evidence of an end product beneficial to the company. Customer satisfaction generally indicates that company units are working well together to produce, inspect, deliver the product on time, and provide the promised follow-up services. Completion of major technical projects generally attests to a well integrated effort on the part of the research, engineering, production, and quality control departments in the organization. A successful advertising campaign, strategically timed and effectively launched, and resulting in gains in sales volume well beyond the original forecasts, reflects unified teamwork on the part of the market research, finance, marketing, and sales departments. An effective recruiting drive which attracts new and promising talent to the organization suggests a well-planned and well-executed program, accomplished through the joint efforts of the personnel, public relations, and principal line operating departments. These and other tests of practical, outcome imply good teamwork—teamwork in harmonizing policies and programs, mobilizing resources, overcoming departmental rivalries, sharing information, "getting the bugs out" of the toughest technical aspects of a project. These and other indications that workers are giving their best in cooperative activity reflect careful attention to coordination.

The same holds true for organizations in the public sector, where managers confront complex problems of huge dimensions. Coordination is becoming more and more urgent in dealing with the massive social problems of housing, criminal justice, transportation, energy allocation, environmental improvement, unemployment, and health care. Despite difficulties with bureaucracies, the woman manager in public service will find opportunities and rewards for her skills competency as a coordinator.

WHAT THE COMPANY CAN DO TO HELP

The tempo, complexity, and competitiveness of modern business enterprise require a company to integrate its many organizational units and to tap the abilities of key people drawn from these units. Moreover, since the company has an important stake in getting its employees to probe problems and suggest solutions to the problems, it must invest, directly and indirectly, in its key managers, helping them develop their capacities for coordination. It must create and maintain a climate which fosters the varied skills and competencies of a good coordinator.

How can the company help the woman manager and provide the desired climate for her growth? Here are some of the more significant measures:

Ensure that company objectives and goals are well defined, that policies are updated, and that there is clear delineation of managerial responsibility and authority.

Guard against overfunctionalization and its hazards, such as bickering, strife, overlap of authority, and isolation.

Capitalize as much as possible on rotational assignments that will bring her to different divisions and departments, exposing her to the interdepartmental relationships.

Provide her with opportunities for troubleshooting ventures, especially those designed to correct faulty management situations that are due to poor planning and control, or lack of coordination, or both.

Establish brief one- or two-day seminars on the improvement of line-staff relationships and fulfillment of their respective roles.

Set a good example for her in constructive give-and-take among departments, since this is crucial to her deeper understanding of the importance of coodinative effort in the middle and upper echelons of management.

Assess candidly the caliber of her own staff meetings: how she conducts them, the extent to which they are productive, and the attitudes generated among her subordinates in such meetings.

Bring her behind the scenes to demonstrate the rationale of new or revised policies, so that she becomes more sensitive to the continuing process of self-renewal in organization; teach her to anticipate revision of policies and programs as the company responds to the economic market, restraints, and competition.

Hold her accountable for results, cost control, and disciplined management of her own organizational unit, and see to it that she avoids building her own "little empire" isolated from others.

Support her when she seems uncertain in approaching problems and their solution.

Coach her in more effective ways of communicating within the "informal" organization, much of which has long been oriented toward males.

Build her self-confidence in handling multiple activities at the same time without her becoming unnerved or frustrated.

Give her some orientation to the importance of "management by objectives" and stress the importance of coordination in providing inputs and unified action toward attainment of objectives.

Remove as much red tape and heel-dragging as possible, so that she is given ample opportunity to demonstrate her abilities. It is the company's responsibility, not hers, to deal effectively with bureaucratic tendencies and with obsolescence.

Provide opportunity for women new in middle management to have a hand in the periodic revision of company's organizational and administrative manuals; this is a valuable experience in detecting weaknesses in coordination among units.

Be candid in your criticism of her performance, both in substantive content and in behavior, on the basis of confirmed feedback on her performance on committees, task forces, and other team efforts. If she is to work hard at self-development in conferring, consulting, and relating with others, a candid critique of her strong, moderate, and weak points will help this learning and self-development process.

The real test is the quality of the woman manager's relationships in coordination, and of her contribution to the team effort. Her skills and competencies may not be enough. The company has a commitment to good professional management and can best meet that commitment by providing a climate for her growth and by giving her the support she merits.

How-to Guidelines for the Coordinator

Some guidelines in fulfilling your part in a coordinative effort, and as a member of the team with other managers, are offered below.

Be sure you understand the particular purpose and goals of the project or program involved. If there is any vagueness, get clarification.

Come to an understanding as to what each member will contribute, generally and specifically, to the overall effort.

Work with a timetable for completion: due dates for reviews, new inputs, progress reports, next steps, meetings, and other requirements.

Anticipate obstacles and resistance and formulate, in advance, drafts of good answers that will counteract them. Question the *substance* of these objections, not the motivations of those who pose them. You can make more headway in counteracting the former; the latter is likely to provoke personal dispute and antagonism. If narrow motivations continue to block the progress of the entire group, expect the chairman or chairwoman or the team leader to take action as needed.

Be prepared to compromise or "bend" on some points, particularly on techniques, approaches, or methods, but seldom on purposes and goals (unless there is some compelling reason to modify or even abandon some goals because of unusual developments).

When other members of the coordinating team lag behind, "needle" them discreetly to quicken their pace so that all efforts and reports are synchronized. When *you* lag behind, have your own assistant or secretary "needle" you before others do.

Conduct most of your communications on an informal one-to-one or one-to-two basis as much as possible. Reserve for formal communication those instances in which a formal presentation is required.

Don't let your ego get in the way. If a particular recommended procedure or approach which you made does not seem to work well despite efforts to improve it, acknowledge and write it off as a "loser" and get on with the show.

Guard against unduly "plugging" your own specialization or functional area of expertise. Remember that you are now part of a team effort representing many functions. Use your specialization or expertise as warranted, but don't press it at the expense of a broader approach to the project.

Challenge superficial measures in any of the team's deliberations. It is better to challenge them now than to run the risk of living with them after they have been adopted.

Avoid letting some past incident, such as a personality clash or a misunderstanding with some individual, blur your objectivity, good sense, and team commitment on the present coordinative effort.

Take the initiative as appropriate; too often a team venture will lag behind and even fail because each person has waited for someone else to act.

Develop a tolerance for error. Mistakes will be made now and then. Errors in a team effort should be dealt with in a supportive, corrective, and constructive manner rather than in a blaming, negative, or threatening manner.

Clarify as early as possible any organizational fuzziness that leads to overlapping authority, confusion of particular roles, or vague relationships with operating departments.

Make sure that no changes or revisions of plans are made unilaterally by anyone on the team. Do battle, if necessary, to defend the concept of joint planning and agreement at all stages.

Meet your commitments as a team member. No alibis and no evasions. If you cannot meet your commitments, you should not be on that particular coordinating team.

Self-Audit: Are You a Good Coordinator?

Do you have the attributes of a good coordinator? Here is a checklist of qualities that you should have—and can develop.

Awareness that your job extends beyond the boundaries of your immediate office, and commitment to accept this responsibility.

_____

A sense of timing in bringing in subordinates and peers at the formative stages of planning and in avoiding the error of calling them in on it too late.

_____

Restraint—resisting any temptation to project yourself as an authority figure and otherwise to flaunt your authority in a team effort (often composed largely of peers).

_____

An understanding of how programs and projects are administered—from their germination through development to logistics, and finally to implementation.

_____

Ability to evaluate feedback objectively and constructively.

_____

Interpersonal relations of a high caliber, especially in the give-and-take of viewpoints, judgments, values, and ideas.

_____

Firmness (and even toughness) in insisting that, once agreed upon by the parties concerned, follow-through action is taken.

_____

Empathy for the other manager's task in representing his or her own department. _____

Communication skill, oral and written, in securing understanding, acceptance, and agreement; putting the art of communication in management to the test. _____

Capacity to take, as well as give, criticism. _____

Articulateness in interpreting and expressing new policies, new plans, new systems, new trends and developments. _____

Awareness that emotions can produce conflict as well as cooperation, and keeping emotions within control when they may threaten to jeopardize the total group effort at problem-solving. _____

Commitment to do your "homework" or other preparation in behalf of the group effort, over and beyond your regular day-to-day managerial responsibilities. _____

Willingness to subordinate your personal likes or dislikes, biases. _____

Analytic ability in dissecting proposals, reports, presentations: separating the essentials from the nonessentials, the central theme from ancillary points, means and ends, facts from opinions. _____

Score Card (responses to the 15 items)

If your *candid* answers are "Yes" to 13 or more of these points, consider yourself as having the attributes which make a good coordinator.

If your answers are "Yes" to 10 through 12 of the points, you have real potential. Now make a determined effort to improve so that you can soon reach 13 or more.

If your answers are "Yes" to less than 9 of these points, you have a long way to go. Use all means of management training and self-discipline to build greater ability as a coordinator in management.

CHAPTER FOUR

The Effective Woman Manager

AS A DELEGATOR

Managing the Allocation of Priorities, Projects, and Decisions

WHAT HAS BLOCKED THE WOMAN'S ROLE AS DELEGATOR?

When the editors of the business journal *Industry Week* interviewed Nancy L. Marcus, they met a successful woman who held a high-level management position at Union Carbide Corporation and at the same time monitored two small business enterprises which she herself had founded. As the interview progressed and focussed on the special skills and abilities needed by the woman manager, Marcus made this observation: of the abilities which women managers must acquire, the key skill is delegating responsibility. She regarded delegation as probably the toughest job for any manager, and she acknowledged that in her case it had probably been the most difficult thing for her to learn.

In her research on *Career Development for Women Executives,* Margaret Hennig made this significant point: Compared with earlier tendencies to be either controlled or controlling, women now had greater awareness of the need for delegation to subordinates. More recently, in *The Managerial Woman,* Hennig and Jardin pinpoint the woman manager's inability to delegate and trace this inability to "overspecialization." Women became so competent at one task or in one particular area that they lacked the general capability required of an effective manager.

J.C. Penney, Clarence Randall, Lawrence Appley, and other business leaders have at various times pointed to similar difficulties among male managers and the consequences of failure to delegate upon their careers. Surveys of "mortality" among managers by management consultants show repeatedly that unwillingness to delegate or inability to delegate well rank very high among the reasons for abortive managerial careers. Such managers reached a ceiling with no future in sight, or were relieved of their responsibilities and transferred to lesser positions, or were asked to resign. If these are the findings for male managers, imagine the disadvantage to the female manager, who has rarely been exposed to the importance and the skills of delegation.

Traditional discrimination against women in employment has

left many scars, among these deprivation of the opportunity to understand and to engage in delegating. Discrimination has blocked both their aspirations and their skills for upgrading into important managerial roles. Sex-linked jobs become subordinate jobs, and those in subordinate positions are generally denied access to responsibilities that involve delegation. This has been the fate of women confined to limited duties in office management, the small retail store, the computer unit, the small cadre of bank tellers, specialized staff positions, and the restrictive merchandising function. Most of these jobs are dead-end lower-supervisory positions. They are not seen as avenues to advancement into more active and challenging levels of management which involve decision-making and the delegation of responsibility.

It is not only the sex-linked patterns of job assignments and promotions that have left women in subordinate positions entailing little or no delegation skills. Sometimes a woman, eager to prove her ability and to demonstrate what she sees as assertiveness, may insist, "Let's do it *my* way." Although this is an understandable reaction, it may also be a damaging one. In effective delegation, the "how" of doing the task is entrusted to the subordinate—after the boss has explained the "what" and the "why." Another reason may be impatience and consequent withdrawal of delegation too soon. This, too, is understandable as a sign of eagerness to show early results. But it is damaging to the climate of delegation.

The most significant obstacle has been the fact that the woman has been restricted from the type of work environment that involves dealing with multiple problems, a crowded in-basket, or varied functions. Consequently, she has been denied the experience of establishing priorities and separating the work that a manager must do herself from the tasks that can be delegated and entrusted to subordinates. For these and other reasons, expecially the restrictiveness of her decision-making role, it is most important that the woman manager develop both understanding and skill in delegation.

THE VALUES OF DELEGATION

Delegating is a way of managing, a more professional way. It is a means by which the manager is able to *multiply* herself, multiply her time, energies, and ability to take on many activities and to get results through others. This is the manager's professional way of "getting on top of things." It is a productive approach to selective decision-making in dealing with various priorities, urgencies, new requirements, and special projects. It is a realistic approach to meeting one's deadlines, since most managerial activities involve time schedules and deadlines: they are expected to be completed, or to be reported on, by a given date. Finally, it is an effective way in which to manage one's time in attaining balanced management.

There are visible advantages to delegation. It helps the manager accomplish more through others, frees her for the most pressing matters, gives her a base for developing reserve strength among her subordinates as members of her management team, helps her grow in the art of managerial decision-making and problem-solving, and paves the way for greater recognition and reward for the results she attains. For the subordinate, delegation has these values: an opportunity to demonstrate ability beyond day-to-day routine tasks; evidence for management to give her more authority, bolster her confidence, and assess her capabilities; a chance to develop a "feel" for problem-solving and decision-making in her department; an enhanced understanding of the business as a whole; a desire or aspiration for management responsibilities of her own in the future; and the opportunity to receive credit and recognition for her accomplishments. Finally, for the company as a whole, delegation leads to better use of talent, supervisory depth when the manager is away, improved morale, sources of new ideas, a capacity for meeting deadlines more readily, and balance in attaining short-term results and long-term goal awareness. In summary, there are a number of gains which contribute to a broader base of participative management.

Perhaps the concept of delegation can be conveyed by

highlighting what occurs positively, constructively in a company as a variety of events serve as input for action. The accompanying chart, "In a Growing, Responding Organization," shows how a healthy, competitive company generates emphasis on the ever-available potential for growth and on the need to convert this potential into action and results. The range of events shown in the chart pinpoints the dynamics of a modern company as it tries to meet economic and social needs, deal with competition, and attain a stronger posture within its industry. To capitalize on these events (which are often opportunities), people and time are required to perform the analysis, testing, and other activity. Such activity, is best carried out through sound decentralization, or "pushing down" of decision-making, as much as possible and with certain safeguards. The individual manager contributes best to the attainment of these results by "digging" herself, delegating the task to capable subordinates available for follow-through, or doing a little of both. These are the ingredients of a constructive management philosophy which fosters delegation.

SOURCE OF AUTHORITY FOR DELEGATING

The accompanying chart depicts, briefly, the background of organizational authority by which the manager can delegate. She thereby shares authority, delegates responsibility, and assumes accountability.

The noted management consultant, Louis Allen, summarizes delegation as involving three components:

Responsibility—the work that is delegated. It is the job a person or an organizational unit is given to do. As defined by Standard Oil of California, responsibilities are the "duties of a position." For example, one of the responsibilities of a chief engineer would be to provide services in connection with engineering, maintenance, plant and process design, technical service, and plant and warehouse construction.

In a Growing, Responding Organization

Events	Takes "Digging"	Needed Organizationally	Needed Individual by the Manager
Forecasts	Investigating	More effective use of information	Substantial blocks of time
Opportunities	Studying		
Programs	Analyzing	Use of task force, study group, committees	Delegation skills
Services	Questions		Building good organizational "climate"
Policy Revisions	Relating past, present, future	Climate of profitable self-criticism	
Priorities			Working well in line and staff relations
Requirements	Assessing various options or alternatives	Reasonable decentralization of decision making	
New problems	Testing out possible impacts		Management of decision-making
Presentations to top management			

Potential	Depth	Sources of Capability
Standards	Better utilization of staff specialists	Communicating
Use of information	Timely and candid communication	Management of changes
New approaches	Meshing of talent —the seasoned "Old Timers" and the "Young Turks"	Development and growth of subordinates
Budgetary views		Management by objectives: planning coordination control
Specializations		Managing oneself as a manager
Consideration of changing or new objectives		

The Nature of Delegation

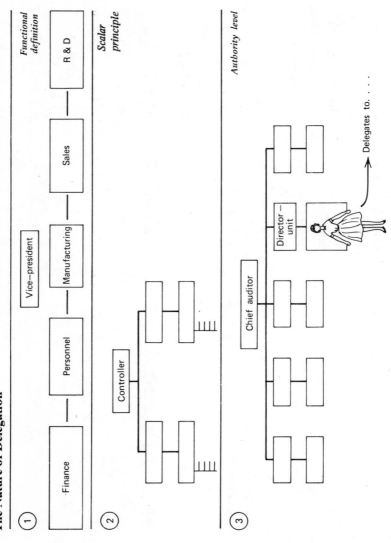

① Functional definition

Finance — Personnel — Vice-president — Manufacturing — Sales — R & D

② Scalar principle

Controller

③ Authority level

Chief auditor

Director—unit

Delegates to. . . . .

Authority—is the sum of the rights and powers a person needs in order to carry out his [or her] responsibilities. Authority may involve such powers or rights as those of spending specified sums of money, of using certain kinds or quantities of material, of hiring designated categories of people. It involves the right to make decisions and to give orders. Boeing Aircraft Company defines authority as the right to originate, direct, act, decide, and control.

Accountability—is the obligation to carry out responsibilities and exercise authority. . . . As defined by Jones and Laughlin Steel Company, accountability is the obligation to account for and report upon the discharge of responsibility or use of authority.*

The process, then, involves the following, expectations of the manager when she is delegating to a subordinate: delegate responsibility, share authority, and assume subsequent accountability.

There are different degrees of delegation. One type has the subordinate take action, requiring no further contact with the superior. Another kind may involve the subordinate taking action but informing the superior of what he or she has done in handling the delegation. Still another kind expects the subordinate to look into the problem, analyze the various options or courses of action in dealing with the problem, assess the relative values of each, keep the superior informed, and recommend one (the best) action for her approval. The latter is the most common kind of delegation. Other variations exist and can be used, too, depending on the nature of the problem and of relationship between manager and her subordinate.

Real and meaningful delegation is characterized largely by these features: (1) It is a "farming out" of part of the manager's total job, with responsibility and commensurate authority to handle a problem and to recommend or make a decision about it. (2) The "what" and the "why" of the problem are explained by the superior and discussed for full understanding, but the "how" of the task in solving it is left largely to the subordinate and, (3) The

*From *Management and Organization* by Louis Allen, New York, McGraw-Hill, 1958, permission of McGraw-Hill Book Company.

end product of the completed assignment contributes to results the solution of the specific problem, to professional growth for the subordinate working on the problem, and to effective use of the manager's time for matters of greater urgency or higher priority.

As shown in the accompanying chart, the main concern of the manager's job is to achieve certain key results and meet the performance standards expressing the company's expectations. Furthermore, this manager must be fully aware of objectives, goals, and priorities as they descend from the corporate level, to the divisional, then to the department levels of the organization. Within the context of her role, responsibilities, and authority, then, the manager's task is largely one of decision-making, facilitated through delegation to subordinates. Two aspects of delegation are shown. One is already codified in the job description or organizational manual; it expresses the day-to-day operational management and defines what is delegated to whom within the entire system or chain of command. In formalized delegation, the employee already has conferred authority to do certain things, for example: to approve an expenditure, to prepare the draft of a contract, to issue a press release, to dispose of surplus equipment, to maintain confidential records, to execute the transfer of an employee, to authorize overtime work, to order a temporary halt to production until safety conditions are restored, or to exercise other specific authority implicit in the job. The other aspect of delegation expresses one- to-one or individual delegation, in which the manager "farms out" or delegates a particular task, problem, or project that needs to be pursued. As the chart indicates, she is thus released to some extent to devote her managerial time to planning, coordinating, consulting innovating, and engaging in other activities.

WHAT CAN OR CANNOT BE DELEGATED

What you, as a boss, can delegate are: (1) *bona fide* problems or issues that require exploration, study, analysis, and recommenda-

The Manager's Job

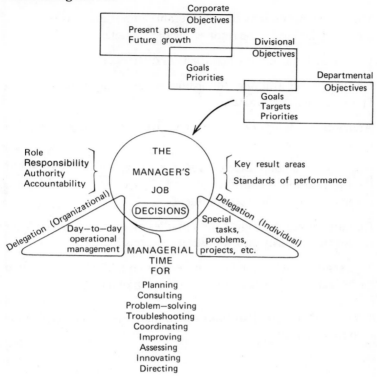

tions for solution of such problems or issues; (2) activities beyond day-to-day operations but still within the scope of the subordinate's job and his or her abilities; (3) projects that guide human talent in a positive direction, toward the company's goals and needs and toward the employee's continuing development and growth; and (4) problems which, if well handled by the subordinate, would conserve the manager's valuable time.

There is no exact prescription for what *cannot* be delegated. However, there is a general agreement on tasks that the manager generally cannot or should not delegate. These include:

Planning—setting plans within larger plans or objectives.

Morale problems that of considerable importance to the work unit and that need to be resolved by the manager.

Reconciling line and staff conflicts or differences.

Coaching and training subordinates, and reviewing the performance of subordinates.

Assignments that *your* superior has given specifically to you and are not to be redelegated.

Any part of a committee or task force assignment, especially if the information is confidential, and that you as a member have taken on as a personal commitment.

Certain pet projects, ideas, or activities of your own, when these do not cut seriously into your larger responsibilities.

Matters on which there just isn't enough qualified talent around to delegate to—or which involve too much of a risk if you do.

All these involve problems and functions that the manager is expected to do herself.

ESSENTIALS IN MAKING THE DELEGATION

Effective delegation requires a kind of communion between the manager and the subordinate. It is one thing to delegate and simply expect the assignment to be carried out well. It is quite another thing to set the stage for it and to build in certain essentials that will greatly enhance the prospects for its successful completion. Among the essentials that must be incorporated by the superior as delegator are these:

Give the employee the "feel" for the problem or situation at hand.

Indicate to the employee that what is to be done should be done within existing policies, systems, and limitations (with some exceptions as approved).

Clarify the objectives of the delegation, the volume of effort that may be involved, the expected completion date, and generally the end product desired in the best interest of the department and the company.

Make known your standards and expectations; provide a yardstick by which you can judge the caliber of the completed staff work.

Assure the subordinate that you will be available as needed at times for further communication, but only within reasonable bounds.

Build the necessary authority into the delegated assignment and make it known to the subordinate and to others that such authority has been given.

Provide some checklist of control points, and arrange informal interim meetings for periodic discussion and evaluation of progress on the delegated project.

Be sure that the individual whom you have selected for the task is ready to take it on and to handle it well—that he or she has the experience, education, training, judgment, or other special abilities.

Be aware, finally, that there is always an element of risk involved, and be prepared to accept the risk of a wrong approach the employee may take, some unorthodox use of data, a flair for originality, or some other development during the time of the assignment.

These essentials are critical in producing a meeting of minds, a communion, between the manager and her subordinate as an assignment is delegated. Without all these essentials, the chances for successful completion of the assignment are diminished.

THE TESTS OF A SUCCESSFUL DELEGATION

"Completed staff work" is the term generally used in referring to the final product presented by the subordinate who has completed a delegated assignment. The marks of good completed staff work are these:

1. **"On target."** The effort was directed at precisely the right problem and with problem-solving intent.

2. **Promptness.** Respect was shown for the time allocation or time limitation set.

3. **Good quality of consultation.** In gathering information, data, points of view, during the course of the project.

4. **Extent of feedback.** Assignment was carried out in accord with the agreed controls set for periodic meetings.

5. **Quality of content.** The completed work was high in terms of:

   Accuracy.
   Judgment.
   Analysis.
   Intellectual honesty.
   Comprehensiveness of pros and cons.
   Quality of presentation.

6. **Action Orientation.** Recommendation was made for a clearly delineated course of action.

8. **Completeness.** Assignment is ready for signature by the boss, or for referral to the next higher level of management for approval there.

Other tests or expressions of a successfully completed delegation would rest in the answers to such questions as these: Was the central problem clearly understood? Were the expectations of the end product clearly expressed and understood? Were informal controls well set and properly exercised—and did they, for the most part, allow the subordinate sufficient freedom to handle the "how" in his or her own way and to be responsible throughout? On the whole, was the undertaking and completion of this assignment a contribution to the company's effectiveness and attainment of goals? Was a recommendation for a decision made by the subordinate and presented to the boss—one on which the boss could now act? Did it save the superior's time and release her for other important activities?

It is important to stress the establishment of informal controls and the exercise of such controls for periodic feedback on progress made on the delegated project. Delegation does not mean abdication. The superior must assure herself of some form of follow-through in the way of controls, and this is desirable for both the manager and the subordinate.

Throughout, of course, the "climate" must be right. The right "climate" is one in which there is trust in the subordinate's ability to handle the specific task or project, frank discussion of errors or "near-miss" situations on the part of the subordinate, helpful guidance based on feedback, and an opportunity for the subordinate to perform reasonably independently. Coaching, providing additional information as needed, helping to remove bottlenecks which impede carrying out of the assignment, counseling, and concern for results are expected of the manager. But candor, firmness, and criticism of errors or lack of progress are also required on her part.

OVERCOME THE TEMPTATION TO "BREAK IN"

The "climate" is sensitive in other respects as well. It is vulnerable, particularly, when the manager is impatient and tends to break in prematurely, withdraw, or cancel the delegation once it has been made to the subordinate—and then proceed to do it herself.

True, there are situations in which such action is warranted. They should, however, be infrequent. Situations like these, for example, would call for the manager to revoke her delegation: when the delegated project proves to be beyond the comprehension or the capabilities of the subordinate; when the time seems to be dragging out unduly—or it has "snowballed" and become so over-extended as to miss the expected time-for-completion target; when informational sources are inadequate or needed cooperation from other departments is lacking, and the employee thus is unable to produce the expected staff work; when an unforeseen shift in emphasis takes place and the project is no longer "hot," or is declared unnecessary; and in certain emergency situations. Thus, there are instances in which a withdrawal or cancellation is warranted. However, perceptive selection of the right subordinate, and good communication and understanding from the outset, can keep the number of instances to a minimum.

The important question is generally not whether the boss can withdraw a delegation but *how* it is to be done. The manager is confronted with a behavioral problem: to do this in a way that will not demoralize the subordinate, and even to help him or her save face in the unsuccessful delegation attempt. Several key guidelines are offered for the manager confronted with this problem:

Be on top of the delegation—that is, be aware of the progress made, the problems encountered, and some of the reasons for these problems—for a sufficient period to confirm that the time has indeed come to break in and withdraw the delegation.

Speak to him or her candidly, and privately—criticize constructively after having provided enough analysis to identify what went wrong and why.

Allow the employee to have some say: there may be another side to the account, not necessarily an alibi, and the employee should have a chance to state it.

If the project or task is still deemed important, and you or your superior believe it should be salvaged and carried through, give the assignment to another employee qualified to undertake it and inform the previous delegatee about this action on your part—in the interest of good morale.

Be sure to keep coaching and training the subordinate who bungled this delegation, encourage and praise other work well done, and look to that person for a subsequent assignment which he or she is capable of carrying through to completion.

THINGS CAN GO WRONG

Difficulties can be encountered in delegation. There may be a tendency to underdelegate or to overdelegate. There may be poor communication in explaining the assignment. Lack of clarity about the expected end product of the delegation can pose a difficulty. Misunderstanding between the boss and the subordinate may develop during the course of the assignment. Needed information may not be available as readily as assumed. The control points may prove to be inadequate in yielding feedback. Or the superior may be impatient and intrude on the delegation without giving the subordinate sufficient opportunity to handle it. Other difficulties can beset delegation.

The most prevalent and severe difficulty, however, is the superior's reluctance to "let go"—lack of will to allocate part of the responsibility and authority to a subordinate. The reason may be one of many: ego, habit, desire to corral all aspects of authority for herself, tradition, fear of sharing credit with others, inexperience, insecurity, lack of trust in others, pressure on the job, the scars of a bad incident in the past where a delegation misfired, or some other reason. Yet, in order to multiply herself through others and to balance her time, energy, and attention among the many varied responsibilities, the manager must learn to delegate willing-ly, rationally, and well.

There are other vulnerabilities, too. Line-staff misunderstanding and dispute about questionable loci of authority can hamper a delegation. Overdelegation or underdelegation disturbs the balance in managerial performance. Another problem is lack of clarity in redelegating to successive levels of management. Defects in con-trols, such as poor timing, lack of standards of performance, failure to establish checkpoints and to review periodically, all are sources of difficulty encountered in delegation.

KNOW YOURSELF

A number of studies of male managers have disclosed the fact that the *unwillingness* to delegate is generally at the heart of the problem much more frequently than is the inability or lack of skill in delegating. The desire to hold on to every facet of the job, reluc-tance to release any portion of the work load, is often the real dilemma.

Managers who demonstrate unwillingness to let go generally fall into one of the following categories. The *inexperienced* manager has made it up to now entirely on her own energy, drive, technical know-how, and other personal resources. Unfortunately, she is deluded in the belief that this pattern will also continue to work well once she is in a managerial position. The *egotistical* manager fancies herself as a perfectionist and thrives on the kudos received for performing exceptionally well. Again, she believes that a subor-dinate will never come close to her standards of perfection. The *in-secure* manager is generally middle-aged, has been passed by, has learned to live with loss of status and diminished responsibilities, and is now just "riding it out." She will possessively seize and hold on to any activity which promises some challenge and might restore a degree of recognition or awareness among the peers. Caught in the insecurity trap, this type of manager will be reluctant to delegate any challenging project to a subordinate. Finally, there is the category which includes the *work addict.* This is the manager who knows no bounds and will relentlessly work on any and all matters, whether they are of high priority, of only moderate importance, or unimportant. This manager, too, will not relinquish any part of the work load except the most routine items.

Another survey of some 300 managers focused on the reasons for nondelegation. These managers represented a good cross-section, both geographically and as representative of industrial and nonindustrial firms. They were acknowledged to be fairly acceptable managers for the most part, except for one weakness: they were generally regarded as reluctant delegators or nondelegators. These perceptions were confirmed in interviews with their peers, their superiors, and their subordinates. In probing the reasons for their unwillingness to delegate, the following ten reasons were cited most frequently by the managers themselves, in the course of the interviews:

My subordinates lack the experience . . . .

It takes more time to explain than to do the job myself . . . .

A mistake by a subordinate could be costly . . . .

My position enables me to get quicker action . . . .

There are some things I cannot delegate to anyone . . . .

My subordinates are specialists and they lack the overall knowledge that many decisions require . . . .

My people are already too busy . . . .

My subordinates just aren't ready to accept more responsibility . . . .

I'm concerned about lack of control over the subordinate's performance when I delegate something to that individual . . . .

I like keeping busy and making my own decisions . . . .*

---

*From Earl Brooks, "Get More Done Easier," *Nation's Business,* July 1962. reprinted with permission of *Nation's Business.*

This same listing has been used and modified in a series of management seminars in which participants were asked to designate whether, in their judgment, these reasons were valid, were alibis, or were questionable ("don't know"). The results have shown repeatedly that professional managers regard most of these reasons, except for one or two, as *alibis* or excuses for not delegating. On the whole, they contend that they are defensive statements by the manager who is unwilling to let go any meaningful portion of his or her in-basket.

The important lesson: know thyself.

NONDELEGATION SHOWS

Inadequate delegation in an organization will often reveal itself, even if for a time it may seem to be operating at a profit. Various results become apparent in an organization if delegation to subordinates is meager. Among such symptoms are these, for example:

"Putting out fires" or handling "crash situations" becomes a pattern in the company or in a department.

Things tend to slow down, even come to a standstill when the manager is away.

Bottlenecks continue and nobody seems to get to the task of removing them adequately.

Deadlines are often missed.

Inequitable work loads develop between two immediate levels of management, with one level quite overworked and the other somewhat underworked.

Backlog of good ideas accumulates needing pursuit and exploration, yet never followed through.

Routineness seems to set in among managerial personnel—the feeling that their abilities are not being sufficiently challenged.

A fairly low orientation prevails regarding management objectives and goals.

A very rugged attitude develops toward making mistakes of any kind.

Key managers are unduly preoccupied with details; there is too much detail for its own sake rather than for use in confirmation.

Decision making is slow, with too much authority clustered at the upper levels.

Managerial time is used poorly.

There is limited interest in managerial succession or preparedness for promotions and transfers to positions of higher responsibility.

Line and staff misunderstandings remain unresolved.

Committees and task forces are used excessively to "bail out" situations.

These and other indicators are often evidence of an organization in which delegation is skimpy.

How-to Guidelines for the Delegator

Here are some key points to bear in mind as you develop your abilities as a delegator:

Know your job and key responsibilities well—and differentiate the "payoff" high priorities, the functions which are necessary but of moderate importance, and the routine activities.

Determine which of the above really warrant your own personal time, energy, and attention, and which of these can be safely turned over to competent subordinates.

Recognize that all delegation is a process of allocating decision-making; one cannot and should not "go it alone."

Pick the right subordinate to whom the delegation is to be made, based on this individual's readiness in terms of knowledge, experience, competency, and availability.

Spread your delegations: delegate to a wider range of people, not just one or two.

Explain carefully the expected end product or desired results of the delegation, and be sure that work does not begin until the goal *is* clearly understood.

Motivate the subordinate as he or she takes on the delegated task or project: focus on the significance of the project and its contribution to organizational goals, on the worker's special abilities, ego involvement, importance of participating in the decision-making process; stress the management team concept; and provide reassurance.

Be fully aware that delegation is not abdication, so exercise controls—perhaps informal, but firm, controls. Set deadlines, review progress, and check results periodically. Raise questions, and be available should you be needed on occasion.

Give the delegatee flexibility and a vote of confidence. Tap his or her originality and independent thinking, and give recognition as earned and warranted.

Intercept a mistake or a wrong approach in time. Be constructively critical and see to it that the subordinate learns from the mistake or the near miss.

Every delegated assignment carries an element of risk. It may backfire, be completed too late, fail to probe the situation more deeply, prove too difficult for the subordinate, or otherwise go wrong. If you must withdraw the delegation in such cases, recognize that this was your risk. Do it without abandoning or condemning the employee. You will need him or her in the future. Hold that employee "in the wings" for a subsequent delegation, one more appropriate to the individual and the situation.

Finally, as your own job grows in scope and complexity, be sure to build into the jobs of your subordinates more and more facets of the work through delegation.

Self Audit: Are You a Good Delegator?

1. Do you have to take work home quite often?   Yes   No
    Why? _____

    _____

    Outline actions you can take to cut this down _____

    _____

    _____

    _____

2. Do you work longer hours than those you supervise or than is usual for people working in this business?   Yes   No

    Steps you could take to change this to a "No" answer _____

    _____

    _____

    _____

3. Do you have little time for appointments, recreation, study, civic work, and the like?   Yes   No

    Time could be obtained by _____

    _____

    _____

    _____

4. Do you need more phones or secretarial assistance, or both, than before?   Yes   No

How did this come about? _____

_____

_____

_____

Plans for doing something about it _____

_____

_____

_____

5. Are you frequently interrupted because others come to you with questions or for advice or decisions?   Yes   No

Why does this happen? _____

_____

_____

Strategies for cutting down these interruptions _____

_____

_____

_____

6. Do your employees feel they should not make work decisions themselves, but should bring all problems to you?   Yes   No

Examples _____

_____

_____

To change this situation you could_____

_____

_____

_____

7. Do you spend some of your working time doing things for others that they could do for themselves?

                                                    Yes   No

Examples _____

_____

_____

Actions you might take to avoid this _____

_____

_____

8. Do you have unfinished jobs accumulating, or difficulty meeting deadlines?   Yes   No

Examples_____ _____

_____

The jobs could be finished in time by_____

_____

_____

_____

9. Do you spend more of your time working on details than on planning and supervising?   Yes   No

Why?_____

_____

_____

_____

For a better balance you could _____

_____

_____

10. Do you feel you must keep close tabs on the
    details if someone is to do a job right?   Yes   No

    Examples _____

    _____

    _____

11. Do you work at details because you enjoy them
    although someone else could do them well
    enough?   Yes   No

    Example _____

    _____

    _____

    What to do about this _____

    _____

    _____

12. Are you inclined to keep a finger in everything
    that is going on?   Yes   No

    Examples _____

    _____

    _____

    Procedures to try instead_____

    _____

    _____

13. Do you lack confidence in your workers' abilities so that you are afraid to risk letting them take over more details?　　　Yes　　　No

Examples _____
_____
_____
_____

14. Are you too conscientious (a perfectionist) with details that are not important for the main objectives of your position?　　　Yes　　　No

Examples _____
_____
_____
_____

New plans to try for this _____
_____
_____
_____

15. Do you keep job details secret from workers, so that none of them will be able to displace you?　　　Yes　　　No

Examples _____
_____
_____
_____

New plans for action _____
_____
_____
_____

16. Do you believe that an executive should be
    rushed in order to justify her salary?   Yes   No

    Why? _____
    _____
    _____
    _____

    An executive's principal job is _____
    _____
    _____
    _____
    _____

17. Do you hesitate to admit that you need help to
    keep on top of your job?   Yes   No

    Examples of help you could use _____
    _____
    _____
    _____
    _____

    List subordinates who could be trained to give this help _____
    _____
    _____
    _____
    _____
    _____
    _____

_____
_____
_____

18. Do you neglect to ask workers for their ideas
    about problems that arise in their work?   Yes   No

    Examples _____
    _____
    _____
    _____
    _____

    To change this you could_____
    _____
    _____
    _____
    _____

19. At the staff meetings which you convene, do
    you find that the same items on the agenda tend
    to be repeated because not much action has been
    taken on them?   Yes   No

    Why does this happen? _____
    _____
    _____

    Plans to change this will include_____
    _____
    _____
    _____

20. Do you find after you are ill, on vacation, or
    away from the office for a few days (travel, at-
    tendance at a conference, visiting a field plant,
    etc.), that your in-basket is quite full upon your
    return?   Yes   No

    What are the reasons for this build-up?_____
    _____
    _____
    _____
    _____

    In order to see that this does not occur so much
    in the future, my plans are to _____
    _____
    _____
    _____
    _____

CHAPTER FIVE

The Effective Woman Manager

AS AN EVALUATOR

In the Management of Ideas, Advice, Proposals

A REVERSAL OF ROLE

It has been said that, even when a woman's potential as a manager has been identified, it will normally take her about 15 years to reach a middle management position. Clearly this is much too long and often too discouraging a road for those with talent and high motivation. The time period can be collapsed very markedly. With well-planned placement and rotation to several first- and second-line supervisory positions, good on-the-job tutoring, evidence of superior exercise of supervisory responsibilities, and continued self-learning and growth, a woman's upgrading and movement into middle-management status can be accomplished within five to six years. The time frame would be reduced radically.

One of the key determinants in enabling a woman to reach this goal is her ability—her willingness and her artfulness—in dealing with ideas, advice, proposals, and viewpoints. The development and treatment of ideas and advice is often the basis for innovation, for breakthroughs that accelerate recognition, reward, and promotion. Mastery in handling ideas, advice, and proposals is thus essential to the professional growth of the woman manager.

Reversal of the woman's role is inherent in this sector of managing. For too long she has been simply an instrument for gathering and transmitting information to her boss. Now, her managerial responsibilities will require sifting, screening, assessing, and evaluating information conveyed to *her* by subordinates and peers. This transition of roles is by no means easily achieved. Stereotyping has left its scars. Sex-typed positions have failed to make use of the woman's native abilities, education, and aptitudes, and have given her little opportunity to convert them into significant skills.

In building the combined skills of listening, screening, and evaluating that are especially relevant to the management of ideas and advice, several essentials must be considered. First is recognition of the need for role reversal from giver to receiver of information. Some women managers will find it necessary, perhaps, to unfreeze certain attitudes they may have about working with male subordinates and peers. Much development of this skill, moreover, will have to take place through self-teaching. It is largely judgmental and not a matter of college or university training. Inevitably, decisiveness will be required in choosing among alternative proposals and ideas. Related to the requirement for decision-making is the need to confront and deal with differences among subordinates, each of whom places a high value on his or her proposal in competition with others.

It is a trying task to maintain a posture of confrontation and at the same time develop a good woman-man peer relationship. However, the expectation that a manager respect employee participation and involvement in decision-making works for the woman, too. As one considers her assets—her greater orientation to personal relationships, her greater capabilities in the interpersonal dynamics of the working group—one recognizes their potential for a managerial career. She should be able to capitalize on these assets in improving whatever leadership style she adopts. Whatever that pattern or style may be, this fundamental tenet holds: See both women and men as *contributors,* each with abilities and talents unrelated to gender.

Finally, one must recognize what is at stake here. It is the growth and progress of the woman in her managerial career. She has long been deprived of line management experience because of the stereotyping which has dominated the world of business and industry. Now, having earned her way to a position as a line manager of a department or division, she can expect an immediate barrage of the problems associated with line management responsibilities. The problems will be diverse and of varying degrees of complexity. The value of sound assistance should not be overlooked in this kind of setting. The woman manager must learn to tap this source of assistance wisely in order to handle the pressures of her new responsibilities. Acceleration in moving to middle-management positions can be accomplished through a combination of factors. These may include on-the-job experience, training courses or graduate school study, enlightened personnel policies within the company, the influence of a mentor, demonstrated managerial ability, and the reinforcement or assistance of one's subordinates in meeting problem-solving events. The last factor, contributory management, should test the woman manager's abilities in seeking, sifting, and evaluating advice.

WHO WILL TRY TO GET YOUR EAR

Those trying to get your ear will be legion. The "chartists" will be intent on reaching you to present their case, they will be armed with chart, pointer, and easel as their tools, and with statistical trends and movements as their content. So will the "manualists," those endowed with mastery of the company's administrative manual, organizational manual, sales manual, or other documentary sources and prescribed rules and regulations. They live by the book and are alert to anybody or anything which violates the book. In addition to the manualists, there are other bureaucrats who are recognized as idea stiflers, advocates of the status quo, office politicians, and vascillators. Not much help from these sources. On the other hand, the visionaries, the experienced, the idea people, the loyalists, and even the gamblers will also be seeking you out. They do warrant your attention, and their ideas and advice generally merit evaluation. The company philosophers will want to muse about the good old days when the company was in its formative years. Expect, too, the "mathematical model" advocates with their passion for the new tools of management: management information services, systems analysis, operations research, PERT, linear programming, decision-gaming, simulation, and other activities. Their advice can be valuable for long-range planning, experimental efforts, testing a particular hypothesis, and other related areas. They should have a try at it, for they have a good deal to offer and the advice may well have payoff potential. But avoid becoming prey to their mystique. Others will offer advice, but their contribution is often nil: the gossip, the chronic complainer, the socializer, the opportunist, and various members of this motley group.

   The best advice is more likely to come from your trusted peers in the management ranks, from subordinate line managers in charge of the bread-and-butter functions of your sector of the business, and from the more competent staff specialists. Good listening, good consultation, and good evaluation of advice from these quarters should generally be profitable.

THE SETTING FOR ADVICE

It has been said obliquely, but unfortunately with some truth, that "the boss never makes a mistake—it's just that she's had bad advice." As organizations become bigger, more complex, and more competitive, there is need for counsel and good advice on a broader scale within middle and upper management. The Biblical reference from the Book of Psalms, "a lamp unto my feet and a light to my path," has meaning for us in dealing with advisers and advice within management. Since to heed advice or to shun it involves an element of risk, skill in filtering and evaluating advice is a vital asset in the life of a manager.

Don't yield to the temptation of shooting for only short-term gains. Take an occasional gamble on a long-term benefit to the company. If you stick to a short-term outlook, you'll find yourself next year just about where you are this year. This comes from an experienced executive, and it was a piece of wisdom passed on to him early in his career as a business manager. Another executive attending a management round-table singled out an enduring piece of counsel received some years back from an elder statesman in the company: When you're given only a two-year tenure in which to accomplish what is really a four-year job in a very competitive industry, you'd better hustle and select the best people on whom you will have to lean—for you will never accomplish it alone. This, he confided, served him well through the years as the company rotated him in successive responsibilities from headquarters to the field and from one plant to another.

It is from one's subordinates, more than from associates or

superiors, that the greatest amount of advice and proposals will come, and it is here that the manager has to learn the art of selective listening and develop the skill of screening advice effectively. To become more professional in the art of filtering and assessing advice and then using it effectively, you must be alert to these points:

Recognize the different categories of advice.

Know what constitutes good advice.

Understand and use the filtering process.

Try "reality testing"—how far you can go before you decide.

Know when to shun advice.

Help your people in the effective presentation of their advice, proposals, and ideas.

Various motives prompt subordinates to channel their advice to the boss. The ego satisfaction that comes with having some degree of involvement in plans, pending decisions, and critical issues is one dominant and genuine reason. The extension of democracy in company affairs, or more participative management, is another. The desire to improve what needs correcting and to attack weaknesses and wastefulness in the organization will prompt a subordinate to come forward with his or her advice to the boss. Personal ambition to gain recognition and to get ahead is another prevailing motive. One's deep-rooted loyalty in trying to protect the interests and reputation of the company will often impel a subordinate to offer advice. Obviously, too, concern with factors affecting the well-being and future of the immediate department or division will strongly motivate an employee to get the ear of a superior. Still other motivations exist, some genuine and others less honorable.

On the other hand, companies also make it a point to solicit advice, and within this management philosophy this function is performed in various ways. Idea people are put on the payroll precisely to originate and submit their views and proposals. Management often tries to achieve cross-fertilization of viewpoints and to this end encourages varied input of advice. Troubleshooters are chosen to diagnose ills and provide advice on overcoming difficulties so that work can be restored to its full level of productivity. Staff assistants are given responsibility to probe complex problems and develop their best judgments. Management's interaction with groups in the organization often leads to requests for advice. Other means range from the elementary suggestion box to the sophistication of hiring prominent outside consultants. Within this range of either individually motivated or company-generated sources, there is need for careful discrimination of advice.

THE KIND OF ADVICE THAT REACHES YOU

It is important to recognize the nature of the advice that reaches you daily or periodically in your management job. It may take various forms:*

1. **Admonition.** A warning, caution, alert; trouble ahead; expedite.

2. **Guidance.** Wise direction to take; delay action for the present; look ahead to the new season; pursue this strategy in making the move.

3. **Intelligence.** Here are the facts, data, latest results; computer suggests target date be changed to July 1; signs that this trend may be reversed; new model setup.

4. **Reinforcement.** Concurrence; we're behind you on this; this is precisely the attack; we'll manage this one through.

5. **Tactics.** Day-to-day maneuvers; here's how we can plug this hole; use extra shift on this job; meet payroll this way.

*Selections from *Help Your Boss and Help Yourself* by Nathaniel Stewart. Reproduced with permission of AMACOM and the American Management Associations.

6. **Interpretation.** This is what it means; the approach is legal; it's policy-safe; it's for preinspection solely.

7. **Disagreement.** Take issue with proposal; we advise you modify it or drop it entirely, too much of a risk; won't stand for controller's veto on this request.

8. **Exhortation.** Pressure; persuasion; insistence on facing up to it; if our competitor may do it, let's jump the gun.

9. **Reassessment.** Controls are too lax, tighten up; too early to tell; we may lose this short-term gain and benefit in another way; let's take a hard look at it this time.

10. **Perspective.** Perhaps we're using the wrong approach to control costs; the problem changes a bit if you look at it this way; it could be expedited, not too late at all; negotiations may not be necessary after all; maybe testing it electronically *plus* chemically will confirm the findings.

This is typical of the range of advice which can reach you as a business manager. At any given time, any one type may best serve your purpose. Even more than one—two or three, perhaps, if you are tapping a number of people—may be warranted. You may have to piece these bits together, weigh one against the other, reconcile them.

The point is to know the nature of the advice you are getting, the kind of "pitch" being made, the purpose, the central theme of the advice being given. It may range from cautious examination ("We don't have enough to go on . . . ") to a proposal for brinkmanship ("Let's go for broke on this one . . . ")

The strength of conviction behind it will vary, too: from a meek "Yes" nod by one subordinate, because "the boss likes to be agreed with," to a showdown by another because, "Like it or not, the stakes are high, and there's no backing off now."

WHAT CONSTITUTES GOOD ADVICE

Advice is no different from a machine or a system. It is good when it works and produces a beneficial outcome. The real test, of course, is its practicality in the best sense. Wisdom is not essential, although a touch of wisdom always helps. Perhaps the most important requisite for sound advice is that it be "on target" and have a "results prospect." To fulfill the target and results requirements (especially with respect to timing, substance, and utility), the advice should be derived from several attributes. Here are some attributes which combine to build good advice that contributes to better problem-solving and management:

1. **Profit from Experience.** Only to the extent that advice is linked to a framework of prior experience can it generally be productive. This is not to say that there are no instances in which the takeoff was new, imaginative, and disdainful of prior experience. But this is the exception. For the most part, drawing upon the fund of experience with a particular problem or issue ensures a broader, more complete perception of the matter: what the story has been up to the present, how the current situation or difficulty came about, and what suggestions seem plausible in facing and resolving the difficulty.

2. **"Homework" well done.** Where the subordinate giving advice has done his or her preparation, the prospects are that the advice will be well reasoned and well presented. Digging into the background, unusual circumstances, the mass of records and other relevant papers, "checking it out," confirming facts pertaining to the current situation—all this is part of the essential homework. Without such attributes, advice will most likely be superficial, fragmentary, off-the-cuff, and even flippant.

3. **Quality of expertise.** In certain cases technical excellence must be evident, particularly where the nature of the problem calls for specialized knowledge. When the advice comes from a staff

specialist in the organization, the boss should expect it to embody the expertise and depth germane to the subject. This counsel should include evidence of comparative systems, critical factors involved, control data, technical analysis of a high order, and awareness of the most recent innovations in the field, be it industrial technology or office management.

4. **Timeliness.** Good advice shows sensitivity to the element of timing. It conveys awareness of the immediacy of the situation and demonstrates a sense of alertness to priorities. Where the issue involves a longer timetable, sound advice should embody a recommendation for realistic stages or phases in accomplishing the task. Or it may be set in terms of early, intermediate, and long-term time frames. The subordinate alert to ongoing developments in the company or in the marketplace, especially among competitors, will take these factors into account. In making a proposal, she will strategically structure them into the timing element to reinforce the substance of advice.

5. **Perspective.** Good advice must have balance and perspective. It pulls together short- and long-term considerations, views the impact of one function upon another if a certain course of action is to be taken, insists upon a more comprehensive outlook, ties program and product plans to administrative support, envisions the ways in which additional resources can be mobilized, and otherwise provides a broader, deeper, more balanced dimension. This perspective is an asset to the manager as she reviews and screens advice which reaches her desk, for inclusion of these factors enables her to see the degrees of risk more clearly. In short, perspective provides the quality of depth so urgently needed for problem-solving and decision making.

6. **Acceptability.** High-quality advice has high acceptability potential. Obviously, profit from experience, homework well done, expertise, and perspective all contribute to acceptability. But there are also other factors: the kind of advice most likely to get

a receptive hearing in the particular environment of this company; its relevance to the thrust being made by the organization and its consistency with the company's broader goals and policies; freedom from bias and recrimination; comprehensiveness; tone of presentation; cost consciousness; anticipation of dissent and countervailing arguments; and other attributes. The logic of presentation and the effectiveness of language also have much to do with the acceptability of advice.

THE FILTERING PROCESS

The manager has at her disposal several sieves. Using them, she can sift the fine particles from the coarse, and she must have the *will* to use these sieves often and skillfully. They may be formal and organizational or informal and personal. The former filter essential information against which a judgment should be made. They provide the manager with a body of "intelligence" which gives her insurance against error or the temptation to take unwise risks. The latter sift more qualitatively. The filtering process generally involves combining the two for the eventual selection of the net advice which seems most sound or productive.

On the formal, organizational side, the following, if resourcefully used, are valuable sieves: staff meetings, schedules, reports, established priorities, regular computer printouts, budget reviews, performance evaluations, statements of progress, customer complaints and suggestions, procedural manuals, and company expressions of changes in goals and objectives. There are also financial status reports, committee proceedings, annual projections, research findings, special task force recommendations, summaries of trips to field plants or offices, cost accounting data, confidential memoranda, opinions rendered by the legal counsel office, and other sources. In addition, the boss is also knowledgeable of changes in the wind, shifts in emphasis on programs, and impediments to performance and progress. By using these resourcefully, the manager can distill the essentials from the less important, the critical from the routine. With this fund of information as the core on which any judgment is to be reviewed, the filtering process will have provided her with the following:

Preliminary checks and balances.

A fund of authentic information.

Essential highlights.

Takeoff for judging or confirming different kinds of advice.

On the informal and personal side, she can use other filters to obtain the best kind of advice. Special assignments, intensive work sessions, private conversations, meetings with leaders of informal groups, briefings, reviews of precedents, visits with key officers, and trial balloons are only some. In using these informal and personal sieves, the manager must take a much more active role. It involves cross-examining, pinning down, pressuring for evidence, digging for facts so far undisclosed through formal sieves, reviewing comments and proposals critically, needling, playing devil's advocate to see what reactions will be forthcoming from others, bluepenciling memos for more specifics and more evidence, and other means such as direct visits to distant plants or offices in the decentralized system.

Through the use of these devices, the manager is able to:

Detect overlapping advice.

Obtain cross-fertilization of views, reactions, and behaviors among her subordinates.

Attain awareness of voids or gaps in coordination.

Distinguish between facts and opinions, ideas and actions.

Confirm reasons for financial stringency, recruitment failures, inadequate quality control, poor service from vendors, and so on.

Know who will take risks, and how far each person will go.

Pit one qualitative recommendation against another.

Effective use of informal, personal sieves also enables one to smoke out the areas of controversy, zones of silence, reasons for withdrawal from risk on the part of some subordinates, intraoffice jealousies, the consequences of candor, and other vital points. In all this examination, the manager's central aim is to sift, from the various kinds of counsel, whatever emerges as best from the vantage point of one who has to make a decision.

Reality testing, therefore, springs from the filtering process, which provides valid information against which a sound judgment can be evaluated. It also pins on the subordinates the responsibility of ensuring the defensibility of their submitted advice and proposals. It provides insurance against rash action, incorporates comprehensive consideration of money, time, technical specializations, policies, performance, and other factors. It enables the manager to determine how far she can profitably go forward. But reality testing must reach some culminating point. As Theodore Sorensen, adviser to the late President Kennedy, observed, there are "limits of permissibility" in assessing the many different kinds of advice reaching an executive.

WHEN TO SHUN ADVICE

Poor advice can be damaging, of course, and the manager must spot the weaknesses which identify advice as unacceptable. Basically, she should try to shun advice that appears to be one-sided, parochial, or too technically oriented; that smacks of avoidance or by contrast, of risk at any price; or that seems superficial.

Moreover, the manager should avoid advice from subordinates who "snow" her with data but fail to interpret the data. She should be suspicious of advice that carries an insistent tone of pressure to "do it now" when immediate or premature action does not seem warranted by the facts. She should shun advice that seems aimed at perpetuating organizational obsolescence.

In all this screening, of course, the manager must know her people. Some of the categories of people habitually offering advice were described earlier in this chapter. In time, she should be able to identify some of the shortcomings of her subordinates—their motivations and competencies—and thus the degree of acceptability of their advice. She will learn to distinguish the overhaulers, the excessively cautious, the yes-ers, the hurried expediters, the over-aggressive and perhaps the overambitious, the logicians but nonrealists, the rank-conscious, the politicians, the theorists, and others.

On the other hand, she should not dismiss advice simply because it happens to involve controversy, a break with the past, or honest difference of opinion. After all, a good chunk of the responsibility of the manager is to be artful in the management of differences and in the engineering of disagreement. Nor should she pass up advice just because of an aversion to people who suggest, "Let's sleep on it for a while." Indeed, "sleeping on it," or delaying an action, may well be warranted in many cases; it also affords a margin of time for more deliberation and confirmation of trends when this factor can be quite important. But if waiting becomes an obvious *pattern* of thinking and seems to be an escapist route, that is another matter.

How-to Guidelines for the Evaluator

In addition to taking a self-audit to assess your tendencies and reactions, you should know how to encourage and draw out the capabilities of your *subordinates* to render good advice. Helping your people sharpen their ability to give good advice takes time. It takes *your* time. It is, however, a kind of investment time—the kind which eventually pays good dividends. Here are some useful guidelines:

Pick subordinates with good judgment and analytic abilities, in addition to their technical know-how and skills.

Be available. Allocate time to meet with your people in order to give them a chance to present their ideas on time. They cannot do so when you are not available.

Develop a climate of "consultative management," one in which subordinates can confer with you as professionals.

Coach and assist subordinates in presenting ideas, particularly in developing the skills of oral communication and use of visual aids.

Delegate more, so that subordinates can see the larger picture as they are entrusted with responsibility for a full project or a special troubleshooting task.

Exercise patience. If a subordinate is not articulate or convincing enough in presenting his or her ideas or advice, give the person another chance to do better. Provide opportunity for another crack at it in a week or two.

Refrain from accepting advice because you happen to like the individual personally. Base your acceptance on the merit of the idea or advice, not on fraternization.

Give recognition and credit, as it is due, to your people for their ideas and advice.

Be a good listener: listen attentively, fully, and with as few outside interruptions as possible.

Alert your people to changing policies, priorities, and program developments.

Get the subordinate to stand on his or her feet and defend ideas or advice as fully as possible.

Cultivate an atmosphere in which there is freedom to exchange views.

Turn down an idea or advice which is unacceptable; be candid in expressing the reason for the rejection.

Keep coaching your people in the art of logical and anlytical reasoning and in productive dialogue.

If there is no outright rejection of a subordinate's idea or advice, and the idea can still be salvaged and used in some way, follow through with constructive thoughts so that the subordinate can carry forward from there.

Set standards. Let it be known that you will not accept mediocrity, a superficial presentation, or a shoddy preparation.

Sharpen employees' wits: Question, interrogate, challenge, and in other ways make them think a matter through, in greater depth and with subtler analysis.

Set a good example in tolerating what seems now to be an unpopular viewpoint on a particular matter.

Treat your people with understanding and dignity as they present their advice, whether the advice be ultimately accepted or rejected. Respect the time, energy, and effort they expended in developing and preparing it for presentation.

Always remember that adaptability is far better than rigidity, that you may have to fight off your own ego at times, that while criticism or opposition should be expressed it should also be constructive, and that challenge is more rewarding than smugness.

Self-Audit: Are You a Good Evaluator?

In this self-audit please check, for each of the main items below, the point on the scale that you feel describes your attitude or behavior most accurately. When you are done, review the entire profile.

The second part of this audit provides an opportunity for self-analysis in expressing "Why" and "What to Do to Change" your attitude and behavior in the best interests of utilizing your people and their advice in the future.

1. Reaction to subordinates when they challenge my own convictions or plans.

1	2	3	4
Just can't take it			Able to be restrained and objective

2. Tendency to let my own reactions, thoughts, and feelings be known.

1	2	3	4
Conceal, mostly			Divulge, mostly

3. Behavior when the pressure is on to have me change my mind on a matter.

1	2	3	4
Yield easily			Hold my ground firmly

4. Tolerance for the ideas, views, and opinions of others.

1	2	3	4
Very limited			Very high

5. Readiness to listen attentively, patiently, and with understanding.

1	2	3	4
Little			Much

6. Usual reaction when it comes to giving others credit and recognition.

1	2	3	4
Very reluctant			Most willing

7. Ability to question and cross-examine others in order to get more information regarding their advice or proposal.

1	2	3	4
Not good. Tend to hurt them.			Probe very well, but without personal hurt.

8. Viewing the intentions of my subordinates as they approach me with ideas or advice.

1 With suspicion	2	3	4 With full trust

9. Usual behavior when bad news, a setback, or complaint reaches me.

1 Quickly angered. Blame others.	2	3	4 Stable. Explore fully. Take action.

10. Tolerance for expressions of praise, confidence, and warmth.

1 Ignore them.	2	3	4 Regard seriously as reinforce- ment

11. Behavior when subject matter presented is quite complex and somewhat difficult to grasp.

1 Pass it up.	2	3	4 Stay with it.

12. Reaction when two or more subordinates, with differing veiwpoints, argue in support of their own views.

1	2	3	4
Rivalry. Suppress it.			Healthy sign. Mediate the situation.

13. Tendency in criticizing and turning down advice presented.

1	2	3	4
Difficult to do. Inaction. Stall.			Part of the job. Be candid.

14. As company enters upon new programs, expands, and the like, tendency regarding participation.

1	2	3	4
Go it alone.			Look largely toward team input

15. Tendency to encourage and use channels of communication from subordinates to myself.

1	2	3	4
Insist on formal channels. Terse, brief presentation.			Open minded to all useful channels. Presentation time as warranted.

Self-Analysis and Follow-up Action (Items 1 - 15)

1. Why? _____
   _____

   Do I need to change my attitudes or behavior? Yes ( ) No ( )
   If "Yes," what to do to change for the better?

   _____
   _____
   _____

2. Why? _____
   _____

   Do I need to change my attitudes or behavior? Yes ( ) No ( )
   If "Yes," what to do to change for the better?

   _____
   _____
   _____

3. Why? _____
   _____

   Do I need to change my attitudes or behavior? Yes ( ) No ( )
   If "Yes," what to do to change for the better?

   _____
   _____
   _____

4. Why? _____
   _____

   Do I need to change my attitudes or behavior? Yes ( ) No ( )
   If "Yes," what to do to change for the better?

   _____
   _____
   _____

5. Why? _____
_____
_____

Do I need to change my attitudes or behavior?   Yes ( ) No ( )
If "Yes," what to do to change for the better?
_____
_____
_____

6. Why? _____
_____
_____

Do I need to change my attitudes or behavior?   Yes ( ) No ( )
If "Yes," what to do to change for the better?
_____
_____
_____

7. Why? _____
_____
_____

Do I need to change my attitudes or behavior?   Yes ( ) No ( )
If "Yes," what to do to change for the better?
_____
_____
_____

8. Why? _____
_____
_____

Do I need to change my attitudes or behavior?   Yes ( ) No ( )
If "Yes," what to do to change for the better?
_____
_____
_____

9. Why? _____

_____

Do I need to change my attitudes or behavior?   Yes ( ) No ( )
If "Yes," what to do to change for the better?

_____

_____

_____

10. Why? _____

_____

Do I need to change my attitudes or behavior?   Yes ( ) No ( )
If "Yes," what to do to change for the better?

_____

_____

_____

11. Why? _____

_____

Do I need to change my attitudes or behavior?   Yes ( ) No ( )
If "Yes," what to do to change for the better?

_____

_____

_____

12. Why? _____

_____

Do I need to change my attitudes or behavior?   Yes ( ) No ( )
If "Yes," what to do to change for the better?

_____

_____

_____

13. Why? _____
_____
_____

Do I need to change my attitudes or behavior?   Yes ( ) No ( )
If "Yes," what to do to change for the better?

_____
_____
_____

14. Why? _____
_____
_____

Do I need to change my attitudes or behavior?   Yes ( ) No ( )
If "Yes," what to do to change for the better?

_____
_____
_____

15. Why? _____
_____
_____

Do I need to change my attitudes or behavior?   Yes ( ) No ( )
If "Yes," what to do to change for the better?

_____
_____
_____

CHAPTER SIX

The Effective Woman Manager

AS A PROBLEM-SOLVER AND DECISION-MAKER

THE EFFECTS OF "NO TRESPASSING"

It is the responsibility for solving problems and making decisions that marks the presence of a manager on the company's payroll. This is the major managerial function. All managers, men and women, must ultimately prove themselves worthy of this responsibility.

Line management, with the built-in daily exposure to operations and results, and with its demands for solving problems which affect results, is seen as the best path to growth for the individual. It is involved in the bread-and-butter issues of direct organizational concern with productivity, profits, and growth. It is here that crises arise, unanticipated problems "break loose," losses or waste are ever likely. Yet a kind of "No Trespassing" sign has long blocked the prospective woman manager from this area. The stereotypes have characterized the woman as one who responds to problems more with sentiment and emotion than with rationality and deliberation. It is more likely that, just like the male manager, she responds somewhere in between these extremes. Yet to dispel the persistent stereotype, it is important for the woman manager to understand and master the skills of problem-solving. Mastering these skills enables her to act rather than react in crises and other problem situations. It is for this reason that this section on problem-solving is more detailed, and cites many specifics and examples.

As a result of the "No Trespassing" sign, women have been doubly deprived: first, they have largely been denied the opportunity to serve in positions which are line- or operations-oriented; second, they have been severely restricted from entering the company's management ranks. The two are closely allied. Since both line technical positions and managerial positions offer a "ringside" view of the continuing scene of company problems, and of approaches used in dealing with these problems, women have been deprived of an important vantage point. Sex-stereotyping of jobs has boxed them in at office desks or in other minor roles distant from the problem-solving front, keeping them estranged from the environment where problems germinate and where problem-solving and decision-making are most active. This isolation has had serious consequences.

If there were more opportunity for close exposure to line operations, women would have excellent on-the-job education to the organizational, technical, human, and other factors that make the main functions tick. These functions include manufacturing, purchasing, warehousing, quality control, marketing, sales, engineering, data processing, accounting, materials handling, research, and other activities. Such education extends also to better understanding of systems, records, standards, processes, procedures, measurements, costs, services, and liaison relationships. It opens the window to the usually less visible but important activities such as inspections, product testing, leasing and rentals, work simplification studies, building and space considerations, plant layout, inventories, insurance, job analyses, price setting, and the nuances of management and union positions in the negotiation of collective bargaining agreements.

PROBLEMS: PROBABILITY, SCOPE, AND DIVERSITY

Modern business enterprise is geared to reality—to its harshness and gratifications. There is no ideal organization, omniscient policy statement, infallible plan, full insight into a competitor's activities, or flawless program. And there are no employees incapable of error. All is imperfect. We plan and hope for developments that will be functional and contributory to the future of the business, but we always encounter things which are dysfunctional or troublesome.

At best, then, we deal with a "mix" of the theoretical and practical when we aim at profits and a good corporate image. There is a place for theory—economic, organizational, and political theory about government regulation of business. There is no place, however, for wishful idealism. Thus we work on the premise that all is imperfect, and that we must correct, modify, and change things in the company to cope with the problems that arise.

The professional manager is expected to sense what is dysfunctional (a problem) and to decide upon a course of action that will remove the obstacle and produce better results. Moreover, this action must be timely and even creative. The line environment is a place for realists. The naive could not survive in it. It is unfortunate but true that most problem-solving ventures arise not out of new projects but out to sheer necessity. Something goes wrong, or someone goes astray. Such incidents are many: erratic workloads, bottlenecks, poor communication, personal rivalries, uncoordinated activities, poor materials, technical difficulties, equipment breakdowns—the wide range of problems that can injure a company's ability to perform and compete effectively in the marketplace. Only a seasoned individual with a line approach to problems can cope with them.

Not all problems spring from general operational necessities. Some do emerge from plans and directives for expansion, diversification, and other forms of growth. Such problems, associated with forecasts, new programs, projections, and other aspects of healthy growth, challenge the manager and in this sense are as enriching for the individual manager as they are exciting for the company. To some extent, women have been involved with aspects of these problems by virtue of their staff roles or positions as administrative assistants to executives in the midst of ferment.

In the management sense, a problem can be defined as anything which is "off target," unwanted, divergent from whatever was expected, and urgent enough to warrant attention, analysis, and correction. It may stem from within the internal organization or derive from outside factors. When it is corrected and, hopefully, eliminated, the department can proceed normally to achieve better results in that area.

Problems in management are extremely diverse differing in frequency, severity, and scope, varying in the kind of chain reaction they produce and the urgency to solve them. Inasmuch as different levels of management monitor their own problems, the woman manager must be aware of the full spectrum of actual and potential problems in management.

Categories of Management Problems

1. Technology Production Problems. Problems in plant modernization and efficiency, engineering design, production standards, machine capability, raw material, suppliers' input, production runs, unit costs, shift requirements, supervision, inspection, quality control, salvage, production planning and control, safety, and so on.

2. Money problems. Budgeting, risk, return, cash flow, capitalization, funding, allocation, managerial accounting, cost control, inflation, union demands, and other financial problems.

3. Representational problems. Problems in representing the company in the trade or industry, the community, with contractors, with investors, in business-government relations, litigation, in general public relations, in image-building, and so on.

4. Physical plant problems. Plant engineering and maintenance, safety standards, warehousing capacity, building layout, reinsurance, security, flexibility for expansion, access in emergencies, materials handling capacity, and the like.

5. Human resource problems. Lowered employee productivity, conflict, skills availability, union representation, motivation, absenteeism, grievances, staffing (selection and placement), incentives and rewards (financial and nonfinancial), job design, training and development, slowdown tactics, morale, use of minority group employees, transfer and replacement, discipline, supervision, cooperation, technology and displacement of human labor, turnover, and so on.

6. **"Intelligence" Problems.** Availability of information, time-liness, accuracy, and utility of ideas and data, statistics, computer printouts, reports of trends, forecasts and projections, proposals, surveys, studies, other general and specific "intelligence."

7. **Evaluation Problems.** Evaluation of unit performance (department, division, plant, etc.) and profit center performance, assessment of functions and their contribution, feedback, adequacy of controls, appraisal of individual performance, recommendations for possible reorganization and their impact.

8. **Organizational Problems.** Chain of command and reporting relationships, shifts in allocation of authority, misalignment of organizational units, line and staff relations, manuals, decentralization, committee structure, span of control, delegation, obsolescence, organization, communication difficulties, interdepartmental coordination and cooperation.

9. **Methods Problems.** Efficiency, work flow, systems analysis, feasibility, paperwork, speed, accuracy, utility, manual versus electronic systems, changes in procedures, economy.

10. **Products Problems.** Styling, packaging, pricing, promotion and advertising of product, modification and improvement, consumer reaction to product, servicing, standard special product, product life cycle, general product strategy, research needs.

11. **Service Problems.** Order handling, customer relations, deliveries, consumer specification requirements, warranties, special services.

12. **Leadership Problems.** Caliber of managerial performance at upper management, middle management, and supervisory levels; quality of expertise in staff function positions; professionalism and behavior of managers.

13. **Goals-Objectives Problems.** Problems of overcoming competition, market penetration, research, goal-setting, planning, expres-

sion of management philosophy, research and new product development, risk, growth strategy (acquisitions, diversification, etc.), program development, updating of old policies and formulation of new policies, expanded resources, business ethics and social responsibility, product selection strategy, dealing with economic forces.

14. Compliance Problems. Compliance with laws governing safety, equal employment opportunity, environmental standards, taxation, licensing, collective bargaining with unions, and other requirements.

APPROACHES AND CRITICAL FACTORS

Problem-solving efforts can be classified as evasive, compromising, and direct. The choice of strategy generally depends on the degree of understanding of the problem, the stakes involved, and the moral courage of the manager in dealing with the situation. Alternative solutions can range from bandaids to surgery.

In the evasive category are the safe, protective solutions, the legalistic trappings that ease out of an answer. They include such attitudes as these: it will solve itself if we let it alone; let's kick it around more, there must be some way out; it's too hot to handle; go by the rule book, don't make exceptions; and, of course, let's procrastinate or do nothing.

The compomising approach, deals with the situation only partially. Some examples: find a solution which will bail you out of a tight spot for the time being; a temporary, interim, or holding action will do for now; this is what we think the "old man" wants, and we'll dress it up a bit; settle for a modified or limited action until the department head retires next October, and let his or her successor take it from there; set up a trial balloon and see what happens, then, capitalize on some of the reactions and ignore the others; if there's a cost factor involved tamper with it, and come up with a solution that cuts costs even if the result is less than satisfactory.

Direct solutions take into account goals, policies, and practical implementation. They reflect willingness to deal with all aspects of the problems and a concern for means and ends. They represent actions which advance the well-being of the business. Direct solutions are based on "intelligence," authority, critical evaluation, and experience, skillfully combined to deal with risk.

The critical factors that can make or break your problem-solving effort are:

The way it looks from where you sit—your perception.

The boundaries within which you can handle the situation—your authority.

The way in which you attack the problem—your approach.

The likelihood that your solution will be carried out—your persuasiveness.

The frame of mind you bring to problems—your attitude.

Managerial *perceptiveness* in assessing the problem situation is the springboard to effective problem-solving and decision-making. "Sizing up" the situation means recognizing the risks involved and what is at stake, clearing away misconceptions, conceptualizing the dimensions of the problem (economic, technical, morale, etc.), sensing the degree of urgency to solve it, assessing the probable consequences if it goes unsolved, and asking the right, incisive questions. An integrative mind alert to company objectives, improved operating performance, and managerial accountability for results will generally acquire a good perception of the problem. On the other hand, lack of experience, emotional frustration, unwillingness to face the issue, superficial reasoning, an overdose of egotism and blind spots (about people, ideas, values, etc.) can distory your perception of the problem. So can excessive technical specialization and narrow perspective.

Authority may be tackled wholly or in part, depending on the organizational structure and the province of your authority vis-à-vis that of other company officers. You can undertake the problem if it is clearly within your authority, if your superior assigns it to you, if there is fuzziness and authority is marginal, or if your department or division has more at stake in this situation than do other organizational units. In the latter case, an alert and concerned manager takes over. It can be said that a good manager holds the initiative. Organizational fuzziness exists in many organizations, as do bureaucracy and petty fiefdoms. One-person rule, second-guessing, nondelegation, unauthorized intervention, and other influences prevail in many organizations. Consequently, knowing the extent of your authority to engage in problem-solving and decision-making is most important, especially in a staff-minded organization whose army of staff specialists often encroaches upon the line manager's authority. In short, *know* where the "authority centers" are in the organization; yours is probably one of them. Fight persistently and strategically to preserve it.

Approaches to problem-solving vary. Taking flight, searching for a pat formula, cocking an ear toward company tradition and precedent and just doing what's been done before, prejudging the situation, going it alone, and similar approaches stem from a limited perception of the problem or a poor managerial attitude. A *constructive* approach is one whose toughness and penetration permit one to probe, validate, and act. A constructive attitude also anticipates obstacles in moving toward the solution, keeps well informed of the latest word in policies and plans, and seeks out and willingly uses good counsel from superiors, subordinates, and colleagues. This approach yields innovative and creative solutions to problems.

Persuasiveness has its place, since solutions must be applied and enforced within the organization. Otherwise what is reached is not a decision but merely a conclusion. Decisions must result in action, must be communicated with clarity, timeliness, and effectiveness, or they lead to confusion. A very significant concept in management asserts that people support what they help create. The manager, then, must engage in dialogue, meetings, and other efforts to allay fears and anxieties and to persuade subordinates of the objectivity and value of proposed solutions. This task extends to one's superiors, too. Keeping them informed of progress in the search for a solution, conferring with them to draw upon their experience, keeping them at bay and warding off intervention while the problem-solving venture continues, and even standing up to and doing battle with them enhance persuasiveness. Articulate presentation of the pros and cons of alternative solutions and conviction in holding your ground until the results are in are also important assets in persuasion.

Much about *attitude* has already been stated or implied. A good attitude in problem-solving embraces self-discipline, professionalism, objectivity, and an overriding concern for productivity, teamwork, and corporate goal attainmnet. Bias, personal ties and friendships that impair decision-making, superficiality, impatience, unilateral actions, preoccupation with the daily desk routine at the expense of a pressing problem, rigidity, fear of criticism, and other "blinders" are all injurious to the managerial attitude in problem-solving and decision-making.

THE PROBLEM-SOLVING PROCESS

Conventional guides to the problem-solving skills focus on the logic, the sequence of steps in the process. Some adopt this six-step formula: identify the problem, gather data and facts for analysis, develop possible solutions, evaluate all the possibilities or alternatives, select the best possible solution, put it into action. Others insist that goals must first be reexamined and possibly restated. Still others hold that problem analysis should overlap with decision development. Whichever pattern she adopts, the woman manager with limited line experience will better understand the process of problem solving if these steps are described in more precise terms. The following steps provide such concrete specification of an abstract process.

Six Steps in Problem Solving

1. Reexamine the goal. Recall or find documented reference to a succinct statement of the hoped-for accomplishment. For example:

Have production reports ready by the close of each day.

Regain 15 percent of former accounts lost to our competitors.

Revise obsolete parts of the manual by December 1.

Reduce conflicts among departments for priority computer time.

Get more prompt consumer reaction to the new product.

Resolve 80 percent of all grievances at first-line supervisory level.

2. Identify the problem. Isolate or highlight the main obstacle or difficulty that constitutes the problem (this may be a cluster of several difficulties):

Backlogs of work, production consistently behind schedule.

Late deliveries and customer complaints.

Repeated shortage of supplies when needed.

Failure to meet sales quotas.

Defective product runs, rejections by Quality Control Unit.

Rising costs per unit.

Excessive absenteeism.

Continuing disagreements on budget revisions.

Among the key questions to be raised in identifying the problem are these: What is wrong? How often does it happen? When and where does it occur? What is the immediate impact? What are the likely consequences if this continues?

3. Define and analyze the problem. Assemble the evidence and get to the causes which account for this difficulty or problem.

Gather facts, data, judgments, opinions, viewpoints.

Consult the official records, files, and other documents for first-hand evidence.

Ask the right questions; the answers will come later.

Use various tools as necessary, such as cost analyses, charts, historical data, systems analysis, progress reports, statistical sampling techniques, personal interviews, direct observation, meetings, surveys, and other tools as appropriate to analysis of the particular problem.

Learn the technical jargon, terminology, schematics, the particular function or department involved; don't let yourself be thrown by strange language.

Avoid preconceived ideas; don't jump to conclusions.

Focus the inquiry on *why* something is wrong, *what* causes the problem, *how* urgent the situation is and *what* is likely to happen if it goes unsolved, rather than on any individual.

Investigate sufficiently, assemble the evidence rigorously,

analyze critically, check it out repeatedly for confirmation, and interpret your findings objectively.

Ask again: are the sources of information absolutely reliable, or probably dependable, or not to be trusted? Are these really established facts, expert opinions, or just display of feelings and emotional reactions?

Examine the entire field of forces affecting the situation, then pinpoint the most *critical* factors that influence the situation and account for the problem.

Summarize on paper the full definition and analysis of the problem as you have completed this step.

4. Develop alternative solutions. Generate ideas and produce a range of possible workable actions, any one or a combination of which might solve the problem. For example:

Authorize overtime to accelerate completion of the job.

Tighten up controls, demand more frequent progress reports.

Revise the existing manual of rules, regulations, procedures.

Withdraw or cancel the order.

Refer it to legal counsel for review and opinion.

Let it ride for the present.

Reassign the responsibility to a more experienced manager.

Question the existing system and perhaps eliminate it.

Defer the advertising campaign until the next fiscal quarter.

Propose to the union a modification of a provision in the existing agreement.

Avoid doing anything at all; it's a "sacred cow."

Contract it out to another firm which can do it better or less expensively.

Change the system to an electronic one since the risk of human error is too great.

Ask for a special waiver to the existing policy.

Modify the product so that it can be sold at a lower price.

This step in problem-solving draws upon your resourcefulness to envision and list possible approaches and actions. It makes demands on the objectivity of the manager in considering feasible alternatives, regardless of their sources or even their apparant lack of merit at the outset. The poor alternatives will be sifted out in any event. The list is to incorporate *all* feasible solutions, from those which appear to be "old hat" to those regarded as "way out."

Summarize on paper all the alternative solutions to be considered.

5. Evaluate the Alternatives. Assess the advantages and disadvantages of each alternative to determine the most promising solutions. For example:

Is it workable? If we attempt it under certain other conditions will it also work?

Does it seem to be feasible in view of present over-all conditions?

What is the degree of risk if we adopt this solution?

Can we afford it in terms of time required, energy, staffing, dislocation, and other factors involved?

Can it be sold to upper management, if such approval should be necessary?

How timely is this action now?

Is it likely to be acceptable to the supervisors and employees involved in this department or in performing this operation?

Will it conflict with other company policies or systems?

Is it legal?

Even if it is legal, will it be regarded as an ethical move?

Would this solution remedy the situation completely? only partially? as a stopgap for the present?

What are the realistic prospects that this solution can be converted into a decision with permanent follow-up implementation?

It is evident that proposed solutions must be evaluated or tested against the criteria of suitability, feasibility, acceptance, legality, consistency in company policies, timing, practicality, and other factors. For the professional manager, this in-depth approach to problem-solving is both demanding and rewarding.

The foregoing sequence shows the process by which a problem is identified and defined and possible actions rigorously considered and evaluated. Now to the concluding step: the selection of the alternative deemed to be "best" to remedy the problem. This culminating step brings one to the actual point of decision-making.

6. Select the Best Alternative (the Solution). After evaluating the pros and cons of the listed alternatives, determine which action will be taken to accomplish the desired results. For example:

One alternative may attain a high score on most of the criteria but be judged too costly and hence consequently unacceptable.

No one solution may emerge as desirable.

One alternative may clearly, and with full consensus of the managers, emerge as the best action to be taken.

The best solution may turn out to be a combination of two or more of the possible solutions, and a marriage may be effected bringing together the particular assets of each.

Two solutions may be seen as possible: one as an interim solution to deal with the immediate situation for next two months; the other as the permanent solution preventing reoccurence of the problem.

Let us say that the manager, in this case, decides on the third item as the course of action. The decision has now been made.

The decision on a solution is the concluding step, but it is incomplete unless it is translated into a clear plan of action, as a written communication to those concerned with the decision. This plan of action should include information on:

What will be accomplished by this decision.

Why the decison is desirable.

How and where it will be carried out.

Who will be involved in carrying out the plan.

When it is to be done.

Under what circumstances it may, if necessary, be revised.

The plan should also include a description of its compatability with other policies (or programs, systems, procedures). The key word from this point on is *action*—specifically: when the plan will be carried out, by whom and with what responsibility, under what conditions and procedures, and with what understanding and commitment.

Although this plan is written, it should be clarified and reinforced with other communications, such as a follow-up oral presentation at a meeting, the use of visual aids as appropriate, the insertion of new pages in the administrative manual if the plan is relevant to its content, and even a demonstration if a particular technical function or procedure is envolved. Of course the action should be scheduled with sufficient time for the people involved to carry it out while pursuing their many other activities.

Throughout this process, from the beginning detection of symptoms of the problem situation to the implementation of the decision and plan, there is much interpersonal activity: communication, the attempt to motivate, alertness to group dynamics, and psychological effort to deal with resistance. Emotions, values, experiences, attitudes, group reactions, and other human elements must be dealt with, as much as facts and statistics. Consider the following example:

Follow-Through on One Specific Problem

1. Reexamine the goal. To reduce sharply or eliminate all nonessential paper work. (This directive was issued from the office of the executive vice-president.)

2. Identify the Problem. Despite the directive, the amount of paperwork reduced or eliminated has been meager. Results have not been good. Some departments still complain of too much paperwork.

3. Define and Analyze the Problem. Investigation indicates that only one of every four departments shows progress in reducing the volume of paperwork. These are mainly the newer departments established, within the last 10 years and administered by the younger managers. The other departments (named _____) are dragging their heels and offering alibis. In essence, they are resisting the directive on reduction or elimination of nonessential paper work.

4. Develop Alternative Solutions. Discussions and judgment point to these possible alternatives in dealing with the problem:

> Request a waiver of the directive for certain offices, because of their unique situation.
>
> Take disciplinary action on departments that don't comply with the order.
>
> Persuade top management to cancel the directive.
>
> Cut the budget of departments which fail to comply.
>
> Put a ban on the initiation of any new forms, reports, requests for statistics, or other actions which generate more paperwork.
>
> Set closer deadlines for reports of progress.
>
> Defer promotions of managers who fail to comply.
>
> Meet individually with each department head to determine the reasons for noncompliance or apparent resistance to the order.
>
> Convene a staff meeting to warn managers and supervisors of possible consequences.
>
> Insist on an organizational survey of the noncomplying departments for an in-depth examination of all their internal documents and strengths and weaknesses in using them.
>
> Hire a consultant with expertise in work measurement, cost reduction, and paperwork management.
>
> Regard one compliance in four in paperwork reduction as not a bad beginning at all, one which other departments may follow later; do nothing more for the present, and wait for more evidence.

5. Evaluate the Alternatives. After careful deliberation of the pros and cons of the foregoing possibilities, and consideration of the more critical factors, give serious attention to these alternatives.

Establish specific, quantitative targets for the amount of paperwork to be reduced, as against the present general executive order. Moreover, set specific timetables to meet these targets.

Hire an outside consultant in work measurement, cost reduction programs, and records and paperwork management to survey nonessential paperwork and recommend appropriate measures.

6. Select the Best Alternative (Solution). The decision is made as follows:

Every department will be expected to reduce or eliminate its paperwork by 20 percent. Each department is given a period of six months in which to achieve this target, and monthly reports are required to show progress.

Any department manager who believes that a unique situation exists in his or her department and that meeting this requirement is unrealistic may, with adequate justification, request a special meeting with the executive vice-president to present a case for exemption.

A draft of a new directive on reducing and eliminating nonessential paperwork in the company is then prepared and forwarded to the executive vice-president for his or her review, approval, and official issuance. The new directive includes such specifics as targeted quantitative reductions, timetables, a format for submitting progress reports, and provision for conditions under which managers can appeal to the executive vice-president for a waiver or exemption from the requirements. It also sets up a series of management meetings on the paperwork reduction program.

DECISION-MAKING AND DECISION-MAKERS

In discussing management and the woman manager, Juliette Moran, a GAF executive in the chemical industry, rejects the notion that women are more humanistic than men. Those who make this kind of observation are making a harsh and unfair indictment, she contends, and she stressed that a woman manager cannot avoid making a hard decision any more than a man. Bette Ann Stead, a strong proponent of female careerism in management, expresses the serious need for this competency: "Woman . . . need experience in decision-making. Since most of their professional activities have been in supportive roles, they generally have no concept of the logical problem-solving process that leads to executive decision-making." Drucker views all of business as a continuum of decisions. He cautions against both the temptation to rush into new problems and the temptation to play it safe and leave the problem alone. Moreover, he makes the perceptive observation that decision-making often involves value conflict, controversy, compromise, and, drudgery in plodding through the many facets of the problem. At other times it involves flashes of insight, hesitation, and the search for certainty where there is none.

There is an entire universe of decision-making theory, semantics, and sophistication. Some seasoned observations and fundamentals about decision-making and decision-makers are summarized below for the woman manager.

Since much business management is beset with probability rather than certainty, there is no such thing as riskless management. It is a delusion to think otherwise. The manager's task, then, is the intelligent handling of risk.

In decision-making, we cannot deal solely with such tangibles as facts, data, and specific events. Important intangibles also influence decision-making. These include company tradition, the tone of recent discussions, the possibility of an imminent breakthrough in research, resistance to ideas, the guessing game that follows upon a merger, the effects of a recent loss of an excellent leader in the organization, an increasing sense of corporate social responsibility, and other factors.

Charles Foreman, long associated with the American Management Association, posits three characteristics of a good decision: (1) it will be as technically perfect as possible, whether in engineering, purchasing, market research, or another area; (2) it will produce as few harmful side effects as possible; and (3) it will have a good chance of being carried out.

Often, the toughest decisions are those that deal with people. Among the recurring and difficult problems to be decided are those concerned with the transfer, promotion, curtailment of responsibilities, selection, and performance rating of key people. Moreover, personal rivalries, "jockeying" for status, invasions of authority, and declining performance of subordinates require decisions that are burdensome for the manager.

It is naive to take the purist view that company values alone are the paramount and exclusive considerations in decision-making. After all, decisions are not made by a mystical "organization." They are made by people. Every manager as a decision-maker has values which enter her judgment on a matter. Norms, a personal philosophy of life, loyalties, concepts of ethical conduct, moral principles, dedication—all reflect personal elements of the decision-maker. With as much objectivity as possible, then, the professional manager tries to reconcile corporate and personal values in arriving at an important decision if that kind of problem touches upon personal values.

Another perspective specifies these characteristics of good decisions:

Good decisions take time.

Good decisions involve the positive and contributory efforts of a number of people, not just one.

Good decisions require a climate of reasonable freedom to express criticism, an unpopular view, an opposing or different position without fear of personal retaliation or vindictiveness.

Good decisions establish no facile consensus or false unanimity, imply nothing suggestive of manipulation "arm-twisting" in the way they were reached.

Good decisions are consistent with corporate or institutional policies. Otherwise you must persuade top management that an existing policy can be modified to accommodate the decison. Your justification must rest largely on how this decision best serves the future of the company.

Although decision-making is a problem, it should also be seen as an opportunity.

Most decisions (administrative, operational, technical, logistic, etc.) should be decentralized and made at the lowest appropriate level or "where the action is." This is where the expertise exists, where people understand the origin of the problem, where the responsibility for results lies, and where individual practitioners and managers must live with the consequences of the decision. When properly decentralized, decisions usually are more qualitative, have better timing, entail less injury to morale, and achieve greater accountability.

All decisions must be converted into action; otherwise they are not decisions but thoughtful conclusions. To convert a decision into action involves the following: (1) timing the announcement of the decision; (2) designating precisely who is to take responsibility for doing what, when, and where; (3) documenting it in the official files or manuals, as appropriate; (4) informing all other managers whose functions may be affected by the decision of all relevant details; (5) resolving the complaints and resistance of those opposed to the decision; (6) setting up appropriate controls for necessary feedback through reports, meetings with supervisors, statistical returns, audit, and other forms of communication; and (7) making such modifications in the decision as are necessary to "get the bugs out" of the new installation or system.

These important observations are drawn from long experience in dealing with decision-making. In her continuing self-education, the woman manager will surely add her own insights.

DECISION-MAKING: ITS ENVIRONMENT

A large battery of tools has been developed for decision-making; these range from exotic intellectualism to rugged practicability. Statistical probability and design, analog prediction, value system scales, decision trees and sequences, mathematical models, and gaming are all posed as scientific approaches to decision-making. Critical Path, PERT, and certain kinds of simulation are other popular tools. All deal with elements of certainty, uncertainty, and probability in coping with decisions, and all are helpful, to some extent, in focusing choices, risks, goals, and probable gains. They also enable the manager to see the business as a whole and to determine the measurements appropriate to a particular area of the business. Decisions can also be designated as rational, deliberative, and purposive; as discretionary and arbitrary; and as irrational, habitual, or random. Some decision-makers operate on the basis of hunches, intuitive feeling, the imprint of prior experience, compulsive reaction, or sheer gamble. However the better approaches are usually orderly, research centered, and creative.

In an earlier discussion, problem-solving was defined as making a choice among alternatives and viewed as the basic cognitive process which underlies and precedes decision-making. The two are very close; in fact, the terms are often used interchangeable. What conventionally distinguishes a decision from a problem-solving venture is the fact that the decision involves an element of futurity, rather than the mere disposition of a current problem.

Obviously, decisions vary in dimension. There is the "one-shot" decision involving a single incident. There are repetitive decisions on matters that for some reason or other are hard to control. There are major decisions, such as budget decisions, that commit large sums of money for a full year. There are small decisions that may involve no more than a change in the disposal of surplus office supplies. Some decisions fall fully within the control of the company— for example, changing workers' shifts in a unionized company under a collective bargaining agreement.

Managers recognize early in the game the difference between the tactical decision and the strategic decision. The former is usually one in which the situation is given, and is generally one-dimensional, has obvious requirements, and involves finding the most feasible or economical adaptation to the situation. An example would be facilitating access to records of transactions by changing from bulky and awkward-to-reach vertical files to visual card inserts on an open metal panel. The strategic decision is generally tied to a major company goal, basic policy, main product line, geographic reach, or development affecting the company's competitive posture. Involved here is the need to pinpoint the real problem by searching rigorously for the right question; determining who really has major responsibility in the matter, assessing the multiple risks involved and the impact of the decision on other functions and programs in the company; appraising the total resources that are or should be available; examining possible implications for social responsibility to the community or financial responsibility to the stockholders; and bridging the present with the future. Obviously, a broad range of factors must be considered, and a number of different alternatives may be possible. Decisions of this magnitude are generally reserved for top management. However, it is increasingly clear that those in middle-management echelons become involved in strategic decisions in some way, and their best inputs are expected.

SOME PITFALLS

Pitfalls, gaps, and weaknesses are found in decison-making, as in other aspects of management. One of these difficulties is the decision "looking for a home"; the situation is one in which the organizational structure fails to specify the locus of responsibility, or in which different managers disclaim a role. There are decision-making ventures that are too long and unwieldy, others that are too fragmentary and piecemeal in approach. There is the dilemma of finding the right answer to the wrong problem, a pitfall arising from failure to spend enough time and effort in isolating the real problem rather than identifying mere surface indicators or symptoms. Unilateral decisions are legion. Egoists, power-seekers, loners, suspicious managers who see subordinates as constant threats, and others who work behind closed doors all tend to make unilateral decisions. Ultimately, they lose out, for good subordinates can clarify, define, question, refine, generate ideas, expedite, and in other ways lend their talents and energy to help in the department's problem-solving and decision-making process. Still another weakness is the fear of making a decision.

Decisions also pose severe difficulties when instructions are believed by others to be morally wrong, too wide in their interpretation, improbable of execution, and otherwise harmful to the organization. Decisions are also hard to make where there are unwritten policies, bureaucracy, nepotism in management, and constant day-to-day crises. These, of course, are manifestations of marginal or poor leadership.

ALLOCATING DECISIONS: WHO MAKES WHAT DECISIONS?

The woman manager will soon perceive a distinction about who makes what decisions. Two main traffic lanes exist in decision-handling. The marker dividing the two lanes separates the decisions in terms of kind, magnitude, and organizational echelons concerned.

Decisions involving *purpose* originate in the higher echelons. Once they are made, traffic flows down successive levels for implementation or follow-through. Decisions that have to do with *application* generally are made in the middle (and lower) echelons. When they have been made, traffic moves upward to higher levels for review and approval, as and when required. The accompanying sketch illustrates this distinction.

Allocation of Decision-Making

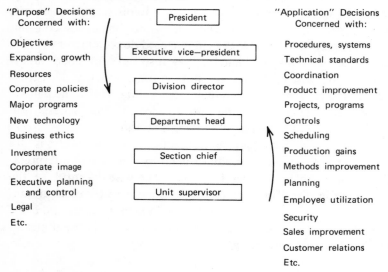

"Purpose" Decisions
   Concerned with:

Objectives
Expansion, growth
Resources
Corporate policies
Major programs
New technology
Business ethics
Investment
Corporate image
Executive planning
   and control
Legal
Etc.

President

Executive vice—president

Division director

Department head

Section chief

Unit supervisor

"Application" Decisions
   Concerned with:

Procedures, systems
Technical standards
Coordination
Product improvement
Projects, programs
Controls
Scheduling
Production gains
Methods improvement
Planning
Employee utilization
Security
Sales improvement
Customer relations
Etc.

WEIGHTING THE FACTORS FOR A SOLUTION

The next example shows the difficulty of arriving at a solution that satisfies all factors. Very seldom can all the criteria be met with equal success. It is often necessary to select the "winning horse" by determining which factors are central and outweigh the others. The situation described to illustrate the many factors is concerned with the problem of whether or not to eliminate the company newspaper, which has been in existence for more than 10 years. A poll of employee interest has indicated that about 50 percent favor its continued publication, 40 percent find it of little value and say that they would not miss it at all, and another 10 percent indicate "no opinion."

It is evident that the effect of discontinuation may be positive on some factors, negative on others, neutral on still others, leaving them unaffected. The range of consequences is in the accompanying outline of factors and of positive and negative consequences.

Whether or Not to Eliminate the Company Newspaper: Factors Considered

Cost-reduction, budget +	Profit statement, in general >
Employee morale −	Labor relations −
Corporate image −	Professional-technical programs >
Productivity −	Legal >
Staff utilization +	Competition and market
Supervision −	gains >
	Space utilization +

A review of these factors discloses that the gains would consist of money savings, better use of a small staff of two people by transfer to another function, and availability for other purposes of the space which would be vacated by the newspaper office. On the debit side, however, are a decline in employee morale, more difficulty in supervision, lowered productivity because of discontent with the loss of a source of communication, a possible breach of the spirit of the labor-relations contract in the failure to keep employees informed of new developments, and perhaps a decline in the company image. Broader factors like long-term profits, legal commitments, technical and research programs, and market penetration would probably be unaffected.

The judgment rendered might well be that the gains do not not outweigh the adverse effects, and that the solution would be to continue the company newspaper.

How-to Guidelines for the Problem-Solver and Decision-Maker

Timing is important; do not delay your decision beyond the time of effective action.

Once you've made the decision, put it behind you. There is no point in mulling over what might have been done. After the decision has been made, just concentrate on the action taken, the results, and the longer-term consequences.

There is seldom need for a hurried decision or a snap judgment— except, of course, in a real emergency. Govern your time well, so that you have enough time to study and assess the situation.

Avoid the trap of accepting mere surface information, data, and opinion. Dig deeper, verify, and don't guess when you can validate.

Make a conscious effort to distinguish between the decisions you *have* to make; the decisions you would *like* to make if you had the time or were relieved of other pressures; the decisions which your

Different Management "Climates"

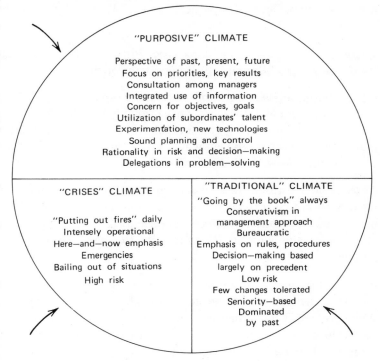

"PURPOSIVE" CLIMATE

Perspective of past, present, future
Focus on priorities, key results
Consultation among managers
Integrated use of information
Concern for objectives, goals
Utilization of subordinates' talent
Experimentation, new technologies
Sound planning and control
Rationality in risk and decision—making
Delegations in problem—solving

"CRISES" CLIMATE

"Putting out fires" daily
Intensely operational
Here—and—now emphasis
Emergencies
Bailing out of situations
High risk

"TRADITIONAL" CLIMATE

"Going by the book" always
Conservativism in
management approach
Bureaucratic
Emphasis on rules, procedures
Decision—making based
largely on precedent
Low risk
Few changes tolerated
Seniority—based
Dominated
by past

Professional managers, recognizing the values of a "purposive" or goal-oriented climate, try to foster this type of management, which is gaining in credibility and acceptance. It has the potential for good problem-solving and decision-making. The weaknesses of the "crises" climate and the bureaucratic "traditional" climate are apparent.

subordinates can make quite competently and which should be *delegated* to them; and the decisions which you are *unable* to make or make alone.

People quite apart from logical reasoning, are the vital element in decision-making. If your decisions are to be effective, you must be alert to who should be "in on things," who should be the source of the information, and when, where, and in what form he or she should have it.

There is no one decision-making type, just as there is no single "leadership type." Be yourself and don't ape others.

Good decision-makers only *appear* to make rapid decisions. What seems to be a fast and decisive act has probably been incubating for some time and has taken considerable thought and anticipation that some day such a problem would arise. Now that the event has occurred, the answer is readily available and is prouded decisively.

There is no substitute for sound judgment. Your individual judgment must not be surrendered. Extracting information from computers, tests, operations research, mathematical programming, and other tools is surely useful. But ultimately, the exercise of judgment is yours.

As a new manager, you may find yourself in an organization which has been cavalier or hit-and-miss in dealing with its problems. When you are in this situation, recognize that it is unrealistic to expect your organizational unit to change rapidly from amateurish, rash, or otherwise inadequate problem-solving to professional, rational, and in-depth problem-solving and decision-making. You will have to work gradually to gain belief and skills in the better approach. Give your efforts the time needed for the transition.

Subordinates look to their managers for cues to making good decisions. You have a fine opportunity to serve as a model and to set a good example with your approach and technique in handling problems and decisions.

There are occasions, certainly, when it is better to defer a decision. Such action is justified: (1) when the delay gives you more time to gather essential data and information that could generate new alternatives; (2) when the time gained can help you do a better job of checking, consulting, and verifying important elements; and (3) when there is no actual time pressure on you and nothing to be gained with a premature decision. After all, postponement in the hope of making a better, more deliberate decision is itself a decision. The main proviso, as indicated earlier, is that your caution not extend beyond the time of required action—that you do not lose your timing.

All organizations have "personalities," as it were. They operate in terms of certain value systems, and within these systems there is an understanding of rewards and punishments, freedom and restraint. It is most difficult to shake off this powerful influence. If you reach a showdown in which you may have to pit your convictions against that "culture" in rendering a decision and gaining acceptance for it, be firm on the *central* point of what is right for the organization, but also be prepared to make concessions or compromises on ancillary parts of the decision. In time, you may find yourself a respected decision-maker, and in the enviable position of having to make even fewer concessions of any kind.

Fatigue, emotional distress, tension, and the pressures of several concurrent problems can affect your mental processes at the time of important decision-making. Under such circumstances, put off your decision temporarily until you are better able to concentrate.

The size and complexity, and sometimes the very tempo of a modern organization make it difficult to play the "lone wolf." Expedite and improve your problem-solving and decision-making by involving others in consultation. Capitalize on the brain power among your subordinates and associates. The decision itself will ultimately be yours.

It is an easy temptation to "go by the book" and thereby lessen the risk in making a decision. The chances are, however, that you will often make an ordinary or an *ad hoc* decision, rather than an effective or creative one. Remember that this is what distinguishes the technician from the manager.

Eliminate the fear of failure, the fear of a decision that might backfire. Simply do your best at problem-solving, be confident of the professionalism you've put into it, expect some minor side effects. At times you can even anticipate resistance despite all your efforts, and expect a decision to turn sour. In this case you will have to retract the decision; do so with candor and humility. But do not fear the possibility of failure.

Your task as a decision-maker can be reinforced, or it can be made vulnerable, depending on the clarity (or fuzziness) of the authority associated with the position and the jurisdiction within which you can take over problems. Have things clarified. More important in most cases is this fact: You probably have more direct and implied authority attached to your managerial position than you think. Use it.

The manager who takes flight in order to avoid decision-making will not long remain a manager. Whether it be a retreat into safer routine and detail, a deliberate trip out of town, the use of accrued vacation time, feigned illness, or another form of withdrawal, avoid such flight. In some extreme cases, unfortunately, managers have escaped through alcholism and only compounded their dilemma.

Above all, remember that the art of decision-making is acquired by making decisions. Prospective managers do not learn decision-making through reading, observation, or training exercises. However helpful these may be, at best they only enable you to learn *about* decision-making. Taking risks and making decisions are the way to develop this ability. There will be errors, of course, but most of the errors, in the right organizational climate, can be retrieved or otherwise reviewed in time by your superior. What is expected of you as manager is that you learn from such errors and avoid repeating them in the future.

Self-Audit: Are You a Good Problem-Solver and Decision-Maker?

Decision-Making Factor	As judged by your superiors			As judged by your peers			As judged by your key subordinates		
	VG	ACC	WK	VG	ACC	WK	VG	ACC	WK
1. Focusing on objectives and goals in making judgments	—	—	—	—	—	—	—	—	—
2. Making routine decisions when facts are at hand and precedents are available	—	—	—	—	—	—	—	—	—
3. Making more difficult decisions where considerable "digging" must be done, precedents are not available, and aspects of the problem are vague	—	—	—	—	—	—	—	—	—
4. Working well under pressure for an early decision on a problem	—	—	—	—	—	—	—	—	—
5. Dealing with decisions that are largely technical, operational, or systems-related	—	—	—	—	—	—	—	—	—
6. Dealing with decisions that are largely people-related (conflicts, personnel actions, etc.)	—	—	—	—	—	—	—	—	—
7. Dealing with decisions that are largely administrative (budget, programs, plans, policies, etc.)	—	—	—	—	—	—	—	—	—
8. Timing decisions	—	—	—	—	—	—	—	—	—
9. Considering long-term as well as short-term effects	—	—	—	—	—	—	—	—	—
10. Converting decisions into follow-through action through communication, reporting system, feedback	—	—	—	—	—	—	—	—	—
11. Showing conviction and firmness once the decision has been made	—	—	—	—	—	—	—	—	—
12. Conferring and consulting with others in gathering "intelligence" about the problem and in formulating the decision	—	—	—	—	—	—	—	—	—
13. Using your authority fully and appropriately in dealing with the problem and making the decision	—	—	—	—	—	—	—	—	—
14. Demonstrating objectivity in assessing all data and other evidence about the problem	—	—	—	—	—	—	—	—	—
15. Maintaining consistency in making judgments and decisions	—	—	—	—	—	—	—	—	—

Decision-Making Factor	As judged by your superiors			As judged by your peers			As judged by your key subordinates		
	VG	ACC	WK	VG	ACC	WK	VG	ACC	WK
16. Working within existing policies and commitments, rather than "fighting" them, in making decisions	—	—	—	—	—	—	—	—	—
17. Taking the initiative on a problem when appropriate	—	—	—	—	—	—	—	—	—
18. Showing moral courage in making a decision which is believed to be best, but which may be unpopular, and on which it may be difficult to gain a consensus	—	—	—	—	—	—	—	—	—
19. Warding off personal ties, friendships, and other subjective elements which might influence the decision	—	—	—	—	—	—	—	—	—
20. Demonstrating concern for accuracy, relevance, full review of pros and cons, and important details	—	—	—	—	—	—	—	—	—
21. Allocating and encouraging more decisions to be made at lower organizational levels by subordinates	—	—	—	—	—	—	—	—	—
22. Maintaining a reasonable willingness to take risks	—	—	—	—	—	—	—	—	—
23. Making provision for continued decision-making while away	—	—	—	—	—	—	—	—	—
24. Exercising judgment in delaying a decision until a more appropriate time	—	—	—	—	—	—	—	—	—
25. Preventing crises in the department and thus avoiding the need for "crash" decisions	—	—	—	—	—	—	—	—	—

Key: VG—very good.
ACC—acceptable.
WK—weak.

CHAPTER SEVEN

The Effective Woman Manager

AS A TIME ALLOCATOR

Governing the Management
of Your Time

TIME AND THE WOMAN MANAGER

You need not be a woman in a hurry to carve a niche for yourself in management. But you *do* have to use your time effectively to gain early visibility as a competent performer. Here is the dilemma: many managers do not govern their managerial time wisely at all; many fail to match time with responsibilities and wonder where the time has gone; and many, won't acknowledge that one can *learn* to utilize his or her time effectively. The woman manager must not fall victim to this dilemma. There is too much at stake.

The nation's foremost management spokesman, Peter Drucker, points out that the management of time is "everybody's Number One problem." He is echoed by the Young Presidents of America, directors of executive development, consultants, survey pollsters, and others. Those who manage well tend to manage their time well. Conversely, those who are found lacking in managerial performance show weaknesses in using their own time responsibly and productively. The fact is that many matters reaching the manager's desk demand substantial blocks of time when there is seldom enough time to do everything fully or effectively. Time is a scarce, precious, and irretrievable resource.

For the woman manager, this problem is especially crucial. She faces not only the demands of regular work load, but other pressures as well, some of these unique to her position. She must respect and use time more judiciously than her male counterpart— for a number of reasons that follow. Her career depends on her learning more quickly about matters that have previously been denied to her occupationally. She desperately needs time to learn the mystique of budgeting, systems design and analysis, technology, financial control, market research, and other aspects of the business enterprise that affect her office or organizational unit. Moreover, she must also learn—and very early—about such practical matters as dealing with unreliable suppliers, facing up to the union steward, handling a discrimination case grievance, appraising her subordinates, and correcting unworkable schedules. Her self-education includes the difficult task of learning the "culture" of the informal organization and the ways of hurdling male-female power relationships in the company "culture." She will be expected to travel and be away from the office more often and for longer periods of time, to return, in many cases, to an overflowing in-basket. Indeed, many a woman manager needs the time to manage artfully the dualism of job and home responsibilities.

In her transitional state from nonsupervisory to supervisory or managerial responsibilities, she will need to resolve her ambivalence about acting promptly on an array of matters and about exercising her newly established authority. There is the constant awareness that the male network in the organization will not tolerate delay, and she must often work longer, harder, and even faster to show evidence of results. In such a setting, the improper use of time can damage her ability to achieve results. She is aware, too, that upgrading and career ladder movement cannot be delayed too long, and that she must show early evidence of her capacity to perform.

The decision-making role into which she is thrust is often unfamiliar. Yet decisiveness and the quality of her decisions are ultimately the tests of a manager. Similarly, the ability to give simultaneous attention to paperwork, people, problems, projects, and emergencies is also a severe test of managerial potential. And here, too, time is of the essence.

The woman manager is aware of the prejudice that women in management waste time in frivolous chatter. She must also overcome the bias expressed in some surveys that women don't like to spend time explaining to others, "breaking in" the new employee, or handling differences and morale problems among workers because she is too preoccupied with herself, her own work, and her own image or importance. Effective management of time can dispel these prejudices.

Finally, there is that constant in the life of many a woman manager: making family and career goals compatible.

For all these reasons, most of them unique to the woman

manager and her emerging role, she must master the art of using managerial time—allocating, conserving, expending, controlling, and governing her time wisely and effectively.

WHY MANAGERS NEED MORE TIME

Several corporate trends and developments highlight the time demands on the manager. The number of priorities in a growing organization tends to increase, and each warrants the manager's continuing attention. To lose sight of any existing priority is to find yourself "on the carpet," receiving harsh criticism in the boss's office. As organizations become larger and the number of staff officers and line officials increases, the woman manager must be available to all colleagues who need to see her. Work loads become more voluminous and more pressing. Attendance at meetings and conferences becomes more frequent. Corporate expectations require her to participate in civic and other activities in the community. Top management is no longer satisfied that a subordinate manager is "on top of things" in day-to-day operations. More is expected of her—ideas, innovations, improvements, planning, special projects, interdepartmental relationships, and alertness to potential problems. These developments characterize the milieu of the modern manager and make inroads on her time.

The manager needs time to think and act in this milieu. More specifically she needs time for such activities as the following:

To visit, confer, inspect.

To "sell" ideas and proposals to upper management.

To make a "crash" effort as unexpected urgencies arise.

To make unhurried but timely decisions.

To improve morale, resolve differences, promote relationships.

To communicate continually.

To meet deadlines.

To modify and update policies, procedures, and systems, or to recommend with justification that these be done.

To read, write, interpret.

To negotiate, persuade.

To identify, diagnose, and analyze problems.

To appraise, develop, and build a team of subordinates.

To improve the workings of the internal unit entrusted to her.

To represent the organization externally.

To be accessible when needed.

To evaluate the feedback of results, good and bad.

And yes, to have time to do battle in behalf of her convictions. There are these demands and others.

These requirements spring, of course, from the female manager's set of responsibilities. The accompanying chart indicates the kinds of responsibilities generally associated with each level. At the worker's level, the employee takes orders, and his or her time demands are determined by the manager. At the supervisory level, the availability and use of time are dictated by the system—for example, the supervisor's identification with the purchasing system, the engineering system, the traffic system, and any other function in which the individual is engaged. At the middle-management level, a formidable set of responsibilities exists, derived from the organization and established to meet special demands. It is estimated that at this level about 75 to 80 percent of the middle manager's time should be concerned with organizationally induced matters. And at the executive level, time is at the discretion of the top-level official to deal with the kind of key responsibilities shown. This is sometimes referred to as self-induced time.

The subject of time management was one focus of the Advanced Management Research (AMR) group, which toured the country

Time-Energy-Purpose Relationship

Executive Level — (Responsibility) Corporate objectives, Planning, Resources, Company image, Policy formulation, Community relations, Government–business relations, Executive control, Industry and company technology, Total organizational improvement

Middle–Management Level — (Responsibility) Policies implementation, Programs, Standards, Coordination, Planning, Line–staff relations, Evaluations, Special projects, Goals, targets, Technical/professional proposals, Priorities, Consultation, Problem–solving, Decision–making, Organizational improvement

Supervisory Level — (Responsibility) Work assignments, Instructions, Orders, Procedures, Methods, Technical direction, Cost control, Review of work, Systems, Reports, Grievance–handling

Employee Level — (Responsibility) Production, Safety, Compliance with rules, regulations

Manager–Induced Time — System–Induced Time — Organization–Induced Time — Discretionary Time

The structure—the levels of responsibility and types of induced time—is credited in part to William Oncken of Oncken & Associates, management consultants.

with a three-day seminar for women entering management positions; the program has been reported on by Virginia Loft. Dr. Mark Silver, a program lecturer and case study leader, prescribed exercises for seminar members in which, once back on the job, they kept records of the categories in which they spent their time: must do, important to do, nice to do, and so on. He found that many of the women managers were burdened with self-imposed time items. Over 60 percent of their time was spent on such activity, rather than in system- or organizationally induced categories. He suggests that, for the relatively inexperienced woman manager, a good deal of this time allocation may be due to curiosity and other involvements that lead to doing rather than managing others to do. (As suggested earlier, the woman manager, especially in middle management, must guard against this tendency, and should gradually allocate close to three fourths of her time to matters under the category of organizationally induced time.) This conclusion is based on a number of studies done by Stewart & Associates.

Budgeting your time with such devices as a weekly calendar is helpful. If you attain only 70 percent of your weekly targets, you will be doing quite well. So don't be easily discouraged and don't dismiss the idea of budgeting time as nonsense. Although many factors will interfere with your plan, it is a good approach to meeting your commitments, and it provides a base to the week's activities.

STRATEGIES IN DEALING WITH THE MANAGEMENT OF TIME

How can you *create* time for yourself? The answer is not simply a matter of dispatch, nor can you budget or allocate time without some clue about what is being budgeted, its relative importance, and possible outcomes of your change in scheduling. Here are some guidelines that provide criteria for, and approaches to, the management of time.

1. Put a *qualitative* element in your time plan. Too often, we tend to express time in quantitative terms solely: there goes another morning wasted; perhaps next week will wrap things up; if we had only started a month earlier things would be different. These expressions of duration are quantitative where it is more important to think in other, qualitative, terms. Think in terms of how well, toward what end, for what value, to meet which responsibility, with how much productivity, with whom and for what reason, to ward off what impending crisis, you have allocated your time.

2. This orientation will help you classify activities into (1) things that *must* be done, and why; (2) things you *want* to get to by a certain period, and why; (3) things that would be *nice* to do, if and when you could get the time; and (4) activities that should not receive any of your time at all because they can be done by others or don't warrant your attention.

   It is imperative to put time where it counts: on essential preparation for decisions, program needs, priorities, goals, targets, troubleshooting in critical situations, technical improvements, improvement of relationships, staff development, and innovative effort.

   The selections may vary, but the thought process is the same for many middle managers who have learned to use time effectively. For example, one plant superintendent of a major automotive company spends all of his *must* time presiding over the daily staff meeting with his assistant superintendents, reviewing production and quality control reports of the preceding day, and visiting with certain key subordinates at their work sites to discuss progress and problems. He devotes his *want to* time to tests of technical improvements, current union demands, review of scheduling changes, and selected reports and data concerned with OSHA compliance (Occupational Safety and Health Administration standards, reports of violations, etc.). All other time allocation is subordinate. In another case, a district sales manager for an office equipment company spends her *must* time on "buttoning up" difficult or complex sales, meeting commitments to contractors, and training and developing the team of sales managers under her supervision. Her *want to* time is reserved for meeting with the area sales director, following through on new headquarters notices and requirements, and assessing sales techniques and approaches for the multiple office equipment products. Again, all other activities have lower priority. Similar patterns exist in the executive suites and in the lower supervisory level.

3. Get to a problem reasonably promptly. Diagnose it, analyze it in sufficient depth, think through possible constructive courses of action, and decide on the one that seems to be the most promising action in solving this problem and perhaps others like it. Expedite the meetings with your most knowledgeable people and with those whose responsibilities bear upon the problem situation, and tap their judgments, views, opinions and dissents in reasonable detail. Use this collective "intelligence" profitably, but make your own decision.

4. Learn to respect time. The real test of such respect is to match time with responsibilities. In management, particularly, there is no such thing as time in and of itself. It is relative. There is only the relationship between time, energy, and purpose. The significant test is how much time is expended, with what energy, toward what end.

5. Be alert to your own weaknesses. One problem may be the way you handle your desk—your habits in sifting paper, maintaining records, making notes, dealing with confidential documents, using the telephone, and engaging in other desk activities. Another may be the bias you show in getting to the in-

basket. There is often a tendency to work on the item on top of the heap, or on the immediate problem. Bird-dogging technical work, work that can and should be done by others, is another possible weakness. Unwillingness to delegate, egotism, a tendency to generate your own tension needlessly, failure to question obsolete methods, blind spots—these and other weaknesses can be detected. Alertness to these pit falls can improve your management of time.

Some interesting studies have demonstrated the significance of personal habits and their relevance to time management. One of these, for example, has shown that if you allocate a full day to writing a report, it will take you a full day to do it. But if you allocate only a half day, you will probably complete the same task just as well in that amount of time.

6. Do not let yourself be victimized by such myths as these: "Some day the pressure will be off and I can devote more time to . . . "; the myth that you can have substantial amounts of uninterrupted time; the notion that you can use substitutional time, such as arriving an hour earlier in the morning before the others report for work and the phones start ringing, or putting in an extra hour after the normal work day when the others have gone; that you can "cut off the faucet"—put the office out of your mind the moment you're in your Volvo and on the way home. Facts disprove these assumptions. The pressure will probably never be off. Some pressures may disapper only to give way to others; this is part of the life of a manager dealing with risks, decisions, and accountability. As for uninterrupted time, you may gain some but not very much, since part of your job is to be accessible to those who seek your help. At best you can reduce the number and frequency of interruptions and the repetition of interruptions by the same subordinates. But to hope for long stretches of uninterrupted time, at least in the lower- and middle-management levels, is quite unrealistic. Substitutional time can make sense *if* you use that extra hour,

before or after the work day, qualitatively. This device may work for some managers and not for others, depending upon individual peak energy levels and other factors. As for forgetting the office as soon as you leave it, few are blessed with this ability. As long as there are things to anticipate the next day, the conscientious manager will think, brood, and jot down ideas and plans. All that changes is the physical environment, which becomes the home rather than the office. You may be more relaxed and may enjoy your time with the family, but it is not likely that you will mentally or emotionally "cut off the faucet" completely. Don't be taken in by these or other myths (including the touted 25-hour day).

7. Beware of the "time robbers"—incidents, events, and situations which, repeated often enough, eat into your time unduly. These episodes are not necessarily wasteful, undesirable, or unproductive. However, they drain off precious time needed for the essential responsibilities and priorities that *really* make a difference in your total performance and accountability.

8. Recognize the distinctions between conserving, controlling, and making time. They are represented in the accompanying chart.

9. Finally, devote time not only to your own goals but also to enabling your superior to meet *his* or *her* objectives, targets, and deadlines. It is both personally and professionally rewarding to do so.

OTHER GUIDELINES

Beyond these strategies in managing time well, there are some other useful guidelines for the woman manager. It is most important that you recognize this truism: you must invest time in order to make time. Considerable time must be invested in the following:

Improving your planning.

Delegating.

Coaching and otherwise developing subordinates.

Communicating and especially listening well.

Sensing new priorities.

Clarifying policies and goals.

"Nosing around" to detect organizational deficiencies which generate problems.

Appraising employee performance.

Resolving differences.

Keeping abreast of new techniques and related developments.

Each of these takes time, but your investment will pay off. Subordinates will become more self-sufficient and will be more available to relieve part of your work load. Eliminating such organizational deficiencies as overlapping, duplication, obsolescence, fuzzy authority, pointless work procedures, and unproductive operations will remove many causes of complaints and the need for troubleshooting ventures. Carefully nurtured relationships, especially between departments, pay off in the cooperative handling of common problems. There is a measure of preventive management in this approach too. It creates time for you.

A useful guideline is the Pareto principle. The accompanying sketch illustrates the way one fundamental goal, attaining results, relates to the management of time.

Although this may be an accurate portrayal, you still cannot forgo many routine, procedural, and technical-operational matters. The point is, however, that you can find ways to consolidate,

The Pareto Time Principle

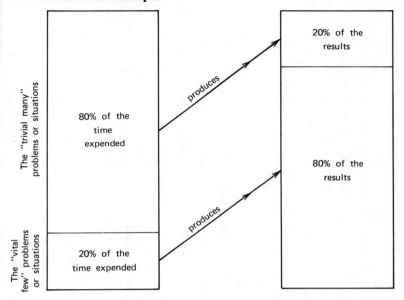

Reprinted by permission of the publisher from *Managing Time at the Top,* ©1970 by the Presidents Association, an affiliate of American Management Associations, Inc.

reduce, simplify, and even eliminate some of the trivia. In any event, you can at least reduce your direct involvement in them through job redesign, delegation, organizational changes, and other management approaches.

The chart on time management is especially important. It identifies and defines three ways of dealing with time: conserving, controlling, and making time. Especially significant are the practical, detailed approaches, techniques, and pointers in each category.

Managing Time

The management of time can be classified in three groupings. "Conserving" time implies shortcuts, gimmicks, pointers, cues, which can result in reducing the amount of time spent. This strategy is particularly useful when applied to activities which are done repeatedly. "Controlling" time refers mainly to a more efficient approach to the management job as well as to the treatment of "time robbers." "Making" time is concerned with the investment of time on broad aspects of the manager's responsibilities, to relieve her of pressure and pay off eventually in very substantial time savings because of the investment.

"Conserving" time	*"Controlling" time*	*"Making" time*
Speed reading; reading for the highlights.	Better, more realistic scheduling.	More effective planning.
	Having secretary "screen" and in other ways save your time.	Better listening, advising.
Using electronics, mechanization such as intercom, tapes, push-button.	Awareness of cyclical periods such as contract renewals, inspections due, quarterly reports, and so on.	Candid appraisal of subordinate's performance.
Drafting of key points of letter rather than writing it fully.		Coaching, on-the-job training and development of subordinates.
Doing business during coffee breaks and the like.	Alertness to deadlines.	Improved communication.
Using form letters.	Budgeting weekly or monthly time.	Effective delegation to subordinates.
Curtailing duration of meetings.	Consolidating dates for travel, conferences, and the like.	Getting competent assistance on high priority matters.
Using library abstracts, digests.		

Good note-taking on new or complicated matters.

Blocking: blocking out time for giving dictation, answering phone calls, and the like.

Using reminders: color tabs, alerts.

Cutting down on lengthy lunches.

Clustering: reading matter in stacks to be read today, by the end of the week, with no set time limit.

Better physical layout to curtail much walking and possible interruptions.

Avoiding "clerking" for your secretary; letting her do it.

Good feedback: knowing who's working on what and state of progress.

Effective, firm correction of employee errors, mistakes, slip-ups, unwise commitments.

Avoiding procrastination—doing it now.

Reducing internal office bickering, personality clashes.

Questioning regular meetings.

Doing preventive management to ward off repeated "crises."

Learning to say "No" to some invitations; sending someone as your representative.

Probing reasons for absenteeism, its effect on staff work loads.

Avoiding perfectionist fetish; accepting high standards.

Being more decisive.

Improving organization: modifying, simplifying, consolidating, eliminating procedures.

Questioning the need for certain functions: do they contribute at all to profitability?

Handling morale situations in time and systematically.

Clarifying policies, program requirements, authority.

Resolving line-staff misunderstandings.

Adapting to "management by objectives" concepts.

Updating standards of performance for your subordinate managers.

Self-Audit: Are You a Good Time Allocator?

Ask yourself these 15 questions periodically. If your answers reveal factors that seem to hold back your progress as a manager, analyze the reasons and determinate to eliminate them.

Do I know what I am really on the payroll for? what is expected of me in the way of key results?   _____

Is the nature of my job and its responsibilities changing so that I need to reassess the activities on which I spend my time?   _____

Do I find myself pressed for decisions, reports due, preparation for conferences, or the undertaking of special projects?   _____

Am I in the habit of putting off too much for tomorrow?   _____

Am I just as burdened with paperwork on my desk today as I was, say, a half year ago?   _____

Do I regularly find myself with "take-home" work in my attache case?   _____

When there are growing work load pressures, am I getting enough relief from my subordinates in order to cope with this situation?

_____

How much of what I do and spend my time on is self-imposed— that is, generated either by a desire for ego fulfillment or by overin-volvement in operations?   _____

As I look back on my weekly calendar of budgeted time, how well do I fare: Very well? Just fair? Rather poorly?   _____

How do I designate the kinds of materials which reach me? Pro-gram directed? Routine? Experimental? Innovative?   _____

To what extent are my subordinates increasing in self-sufficiency to work on their own problems and make their own decisions without drawing upon my time to assist them? _____

How well do I know my own physical energy, ability to concentrate, habits at the desk, and physical and mental peaks so that I can work on difficult or complex matters when I'm best able to? Very well? To some degree? Not well? _____

What is the condition of my desk, vertical files, records, and other essential information needed at hand? Very orderly? Fair but backlogged at times? Messy, inaccessible? _____

Do I find myself engaged in "socializing" too much? Are extended telephone conversations, long visits with other managers and colleagues, late luncheons, and the like, habitual in my schedule?

_____

Am I over extended in committee or other group activity, thus spending far more time than I can afford to on meetings, conferences, and similar commitments? _____

Follow-Up Project: Dealing with "Time Robbers"

A "time robber" is an event, incident, or situation that, if repeated often or with some frequency, tends to eat into your time unduly. It is not necessarily wasteful or undesirable. You wish, however, that it didn't eat into your managerial time— time that you could use more profitably for more significant aspects of your job.
   Review the list of typical time robbers given below.

1.   Identify two or three time robbers that affect your job and your time management.

2.   Indicate what you have done, attempted to do, or plan to do to deal with these time robbers.

3. Talk to friends in management or with your own manager to find out what *they* might have done to deal successfully with these "time robbers."

Time Robbers

Meetings.

Correspondence.

Visitors.

Reports.

Travel (official trips).

Questionnaires, and the like.

Committee work.

Gripes, complaints, morale situations.

Inaccessible records.

Searches for needed information.

Emergency situations, troubleshooting.

Overinvolvement in personal problems of a subordinate.

Telephone.

Appointments—late arrivals, cancellations.

Subordinates needing attention.

Attempts to reach other managers for consultation.

Need for discussion and correction of inadequate work by subordinates.

"Breaking in" of new employees.

Community activities.

"Standing by" for scheduled meetings with bosses or other managers.

Clarifications of misunderstandings of policies, instructions, and the like.

New projects which seem to "break in" on the work load.

Other time robbers.

CHAPTER EIGHT

The Effective Woman Manager

AS A TRAINER AND GUIDE

Developing the Human Resources of Your Staff

WHY DEVELOP SUBORDINATES?
YOUR HUMAN RESOURCES

Growth breeds growth. There is a chain reaction in which the manager's growth produces development in her subordinates. The reverse is also true, for highly competent and aspiring subordinates goad their superiors on to greater accomplishments. And as they grow, so invariably, does the company, grow and prosper. Each achievement, goal attained, successful program and breakthrough nourishes all contributors: subordinates, manangers, and the company. In the more progressive organizations the objectives of the company, the responsibilities of the manager, and the career interests of subordinates tend to mesh well. This is a paramount reason for you to develop your human resources.

A progressive company is always concerned with expansion and with managerial succession: filling new key management slots. Who is to replace the manager about to move up the ladder? If no one is ready, the company may defer or cancel a planned promotion or hire an outsider. Many have been known to resort to these moves. However, most companies prefer to make promotions from within to the extent possible. Some of your subordinates may be prospective candidates for promotion—if their abilities have been sufficiently developed. Moreover, you as manager have defaulted on one of your responsibilities if there is no evidence of managerial succession in your department.

Personnel development is also suggested by the very features of good management that we constantly look for: a better corps of managers and supervisors; improved productivity at all levels and by all subordinates; good relationships and teamwork among different departments and functions; improved communication, upward, lateral, and downward; greater customer and client satisfaction with products and services; improved competitive standing within the industry—in market penetration, product acceptance, and profits. All, obviously, are tied to human talent and superior performance; yet in order to reach these goals, we need a reservoir of talent among subordinates, talent and abilities that contribute to both the present needs and the future expectations of the company.

It is widely recognized that the manager has the responsibility to create the conditions for staff development, a "climate" in which aspiring subordinates can achieve the most for the company and at the same time develop fully. Development, therefore is a two- pronged matter: it involves both directed development of the subordinate by the manager, and self-development on the part of the individual in his or her own behalf.

The increasing emphasis on mutuality itself explains why the manager should develop her subordinates' ability. As behavioral science increasingly influences business management thinking, these needs become evident: mutual concern for objectives and goals; mutual knowledge of plans, policies, priorities, and new developments; mutual determination to solve problems and overcome organizational difficulties; mutual responsibility for performance and its effects; and mutual commitment to the purposes and the future well-being of the organization. To achieve this mutuality is no easy task, for the ideal must be translated into the practical. As a manager enhances her subordinates' understanding and capabilities, another step forward is taken in attaining mutuality in practice.

Rationality is not enough, however, to justify the need for staff development. In the end the manager must deal with herself, in terms of her emotions, doubts, values, and convictions. She must *feel* and *believe* that the development of subordinates is in her own interests and those of the company. She must be prepared to live philosophically with the realization that, after having developed her people, she will lose some of this excellent talent to other departments. Her only solace will be the reputation she gains as a dedicated and successful nurturer of talent and the reputation she gives her department as a recognized breeding ground for "comers" in the company. Above all, she will have to shake off the fear that every competent and ambitious employee is a threat to her own job security. All these factors must be grappled with if the manager is to persuade herself to devote her time and energy to the development of human resources—her own subordinates.

EXPOSURE TO HUMAN RESOURCES MANAGEMENT

Compared with her counterpart, the male manager, the woman manager is neither at an advantage nor disadvantage in human resources management. Both, as supervisors, have probably had a great deal of exposure in *dealing* with people—in interviewing and hiring staff, handling complaints and grievances, reviewing requests for transfers, training new workers, counseling problem employees, disciplining negligent workers, firing incompetents, communicating instructions, explaining organizational changes and new policies, curbing harmful rumors, facing up to union stewards, and working with human situations in other ways.

Neither, however, has probably had broad experience in *developing* and activating human resources. We have generally not done very well in motivating subordinates, improving the morale of the work group, eliciting participation, broadening opportunities for more challenging assignments, providing constructive feedback helpful to employees' careers, assessing their potential, providing a climate conducive to productivity, building effective work teams, or training promising individuals for more complex responsibilities. To be sure, much of this activity has been, and currently is, carried out in many companies and in a cross-section of industries—but seldom as a conscious, deliberate, and continuing practice. There is a long way to go, and this backwardness in an important area accounts for the recent emergence of the human resources management movement in American business enterprise.

In other respects, there may be disadvantages to the woman manager. One handicap involves opportunities for management training. Male managers have for many years been exposed to management training seminars, conferences, courses, and other programs focusing on the manager's role in developing key subordinates and in building strong work teams. Women have been denied these educational opportunities. For years very few, if any, women were seen among the registrants or conferees in these programs. Fortunately, there is now increasing evidence of change.

Another inherent disadvantage had to do with the often isolated position of the woman. Often she has served as secretarial assistant, staff specialist, aide, or office manager in a reporting relationship to one man. Except, perhaps, for being in the presence of one or more clerks and stenographers, she has been isolated from the environment in which human resources are used at large. Even in many supervisory positions in the retail merchandising store, bank, laboratory, editorial office, company library, fashion design studio, or other locale, she has lacked exposure to the ways of developing coordinated worker activity. She has not worked in the area of manufacturing, marketing, or sales, or in other major sectors of the company.

Moreover, it would not be wrong to say that many a woman supervisor, seeing advancement and promotions going mainly to men, had to be concerned with her own security and well-being in a work culture that discriminated against her sex, and could understandably be quite indifferent to the development and career growth of her subordinates. However, sweeping changes have taken place in the culture of the work environment, and both the need and the opportunity exist for the woman manager to gain experience and expertise in human resources management. It is an essential skill to be mastered.

HUMAN REOSURCES IN THE ORGANIZATION

All companies, whatever their industry and their product, are in the "people business" just as they are in the "idea business." Those failing to recognize this fact soon find themselves unable to compete in the marketplace. They lose their economic base and ultimately fall by the wayside. The companies that survive are the ones that develop and tap the potential of their employees and keep building a strong reserve of human talent for the future.

Managers in these companies are entrusted with human assets, and they are expected to work cooperatively with the personnel department in a joint effort to attract, motivate, use, and retain these assets. Thus, every manager is expected to be a developer of people: a trainer, guide, coach, or mentor of the workers under her supervision.

Work occurs within a human context. The ability to carry out projects with and through people is a test of one's competence as a manager. Drucker refers to the manager as one who must integrate not only "sideways," with those in other functions, but also "downward" with her own people in the direct manager-employee relationship. More than 20 years ago Robert Katz, writing for the *Harvard Business Review* on the skills of an effective manager, cited three basic skills: *technical skill* in one's area of specialization; *human skill* in building relationships, particularly, cooperative effort in the team one leads; and *conceptual skill* in perceiving the corporate enterprise as a whole and the influences that affects its policies, risks, and decisions. It is acknowledged, after many years, that human skill is still the most difficult to develop and to practice effectively. Yet human skill is often held to be the most essential of the skills the manager must acquire.

The uniqueness of the human resource, and the challenge and opportunity it presents for management action, is best expressed by Ray Killian, vice-president and director of personnel and public relations of one of the nation's largest department store chains. He makes his point tersely, but realistically and forcefully:

The human resource has these characteristics:

It cannot be purchased *en masse,* but individually—one person at a time.

It cannot be hoarded or warehoused, but it must be made available on an hourly and daily basis.

It is perishable in that it must be used currently; if it is not needed or if it is unproductive today, it is still consumed.

The company must, through its reputation and efforts, solicit the human resource.

Each individual has the option not to apply for a job, not to report for work each day, and not to expend effort.

The company must, through its organization and programs, merit the presence and contribution of the human resource.

The individual has the freedom to resign, and the company has certain options for discharging the individual. Thus the relationship is fragile, with each party having the right to terminate it.

The human resource represents both short- and long-range investment on the part of the company, an investment in which the profitability and life span are unpredictable.

The availability of the human resource, its contribution, and its return on investment depend on appropriate attention and response by management.

The burden is on those people who control and operate the company to recognize the uniqueness of this resource and to deserve its presence and full commitment.*

This is the nature of human resources in organization. The manager has a responsibility to develop, motivate, use, and recognize the talents and abilities of her subordinates.

LEADING YOUR HUMAN RESOURCES

As a trainer and guide, the manager must know the paths to follow in developing her subordinates. These are the main routes for the manager trying to build a team of subordinates.

---

*From Ray A. Killian, *Human Resources in Management: An ROI Approach.* New York: AMACOM, *American Management Associations,* 1976, p. 8. Reprinted with permission of AMACOM and American Management Associations.

1. Set clear goals, so that subordinates are fully aware of the company's larger objectives, the goals and priorities of the division as it contributes to overall company objectives, and the time parameters involved in attaining these goals.

2. Clarify the individual's duties, responsibilities, and authority, and the dimensions of his or her job, particularly as the nature of the job changes.

3. Formulate realistic, attainable standards of performance for the individual, explaining explicitly what is required to measure up to the job.

4. Provide the kind of on-the-job training, coaching, and counseling which really motivates the subordinate and enables him or her to grow in technical competence, interpersonal relations, and problem-solving ability.

5. Evaluate objectively the performance and results actually attained by the individual against the established standards of performance, and provide feedback of constructive criticism and advice on his or her strengths and weaknesses as an employee.

6. Cultivate the kind of organizational climate most conducive to individual productivity, team morale, and effective contribution to established goals.

These roads should not be traveled alone. To the extent possible, top management should sanction and encourage the concept of developing subordinates. Top management should see this effort as a kind of capital investment, similar to investments in technology, research, plant sites, and other kinds of capital investment with potential future payoff in the economic interests of the company. Employee development should also to be supported by the personnel department in its programs and policies. It should be reinforced through imaginative recruitment of new staff, effective screening to match qualifications and jobs, a sound compensation system, fair employment practices, a performance appraisal program that commands credibility, career opportunities, assessment centers, incentives for additional education and training, a set of sound policies governing transfers and promotions, and other elements that make up an effective, modern personnel management program. Without the support of top management and the personnel department, the line manager will obviously have a difficult road to travel alone.

Many volumes have been published on the ways of developing human resources. There are also many works on the managerial role in the development of subordinates. In her continuing self-education, the woman manager should read some of these sources. Among those of practical value are James Cribbin's *Effective Managerial Leadership,* Max Wortman and Joann Sperling's *Defining the Manager's Job,* Charles Hughes' *Goal Setting,* and Marion Kellogg's *Closing the Performance Gap.*

PERFORMANCE STANDARDS

A broad overview of some of these routes is appropriate at this point. More detailed treatment will be given to the particular responsibility of coaching, motivating, counseling, and otherwise developing subordinates. Goal-setting is a process in which there is joint deliberation and agreement between boss and subordinate in determining the special task to be undertaken (over and beyond the daily routine operations) and the particular contribution each one will make to its accomplishment. Goal-setting also involves agreement on the target completion date, the resources required for input and support, the plan of work, periodic reviews of progress and problems, and the measurement of final results against the goal. Goals are set high enough to encourage excellence yet not so high as to be unattainable. Thus, there is a great need to stretch the subordinate's analytic abilities, judgment, technical knowhow, initiative, and independent effort in solving problems and in making certain decisions. Periodic review provides the subordinate with adequate feedback on how well he or she is doing, on aspects requiring assistance or advice from the manager, and particularly on areas in which he or she must gain greater understanding and perspective and strengthen specific skills that are now marginal or no more than adequate.

Formulating performance standards for the subordinate's job is a must. This has always been a troublesome part of the manager's task because much time, depth analysis, and rigorous effort are entailed in formulating and expressing such standards in writing— and particularly in gaining the subordinate's acceptance of these standards as understandable, fair, and attainable measures of performance. The development of criteria of evaluation is often deferred by the busy manager precisely because of the difficulty involved. Nevertheless, it must be done, for it is an essential management tool. Despite the painstaking effort and time required for analysis and consultation, there are several approaches by which this task can be expedited. The standards can be formulated by the manager herself, one job at a time, especially in the case of a new job to be written up or an existing job about to be filled by a new incumbent. Or the standards can be developed by the subordinate, who takes on this arduous task and submits a draft of proposed standards for his or her own job, to be reviewed and modified as necessary by the boss. The project can also be undertaken as a joint effort, a very desirable alternative which enables both the boss and the subordinate to engage in analysis, express their views at each point, and confer to mediate any serious differences. It results in better mutual understanding of the final standards that emerge from the joint endeavor. Sometimes standards of performance can be formulated tentatively and tested experimentally. Judgment is then made, on the basis of the findings, on whether the standards are too soft, are fair, or are excessive. Another approach is to use special staff assistance to do some of the leg work in analyzing the job components and in drafting proposed standards. At times one can ask that the standards be developed by an affected group (for example, salesmen, purchasing agents, auditors) who perform roughly the same jobs, and who can devise common standards applicable to all in that group. Quite often, managers do the job the easy way, albeit with vulnerability, by basing standards on precedent—on the standards which have been historically acceptable over the years, with only occasional and minor revision.

Some managers, especially new or relatively inexperienced managers, tend to confuse job descriptions with performance standards. The job description simply documents *what* the job entails in terms of duties, tasks, and responsibilities, so that the employee knows his or her role and functions in the organization. Performance standards specify the criteria for gauging *how well* the job is done, the tests for determining acceptable performance. A safety director knows from the job description the duties involved in promoting a safety program, conducting safety inspections, submitting safety reports, and checking on the purchase of equipment that is free of injury hazards. Performance standards express how well he or she is doing with respect to frequency of accidents, severity of the accidents, reviewing injury compensation claims, handling disciplinary cases that involve employee negligence in areas relative to safety, reducing accidents, gaining cooperation from managers of line departments (for example, in production and warehousing), and so on.

Standards become meaningful only to the extent that they provide specifications, criteria, or indicators for gauging results. Thus, a good standard of performance should have built into it such measurable criteria as these:

How soon? by when?
At what cost?
With what accuracy?
How much?
With what impact?

In what manner?
With what degree of professionalism?
How productive?
How innovative?
With what gains?

If a standard cannot be quantified, it should at least be capable of being verbalized clearly. In this respect, it is helpful to evaluate a subordinate's performance in terms of any one or a combination of these:

Time factors.
Quality factors.
Morale factors.
Safety factors.
Cost factors.
Volume or output factors.
Public relations factors.
Customer satisfaction factors.
Improvement factors.
Profit factors.
Other relevant factors.

Above all, standards should be well formulated, attainable, well documented, and applicable for evaluating employee performance. They should also be subject to review and revision when they seem unacceptable because of changes or forces beyond the control of the employee and his or her superior.

APPRAISING SUBORDINATES

Appraising or rating your subordinates' performance under the company's formal appraisal system is another essential. Again, many managers find this task to be uncomfortable or demanding.

Many reasons are given by managers to rationalize their evasion of this task. They claim that they do not want to "play God" in judging men or women and in influencing their lives and their futures. They contend that no system of evaluation is sufficiently objective, and that since systems are imperfect it is better not to use them. They argue that it is only an assumption that people want to develop, grow, compete, or improve, that workers are quite indifferent to their superior's evaluation as long as their salaries and fringe benefits are not adversely affected. Still others find it difficult to "level" with a subordinate for fear of disrupting their relaxed daily relationships. At times they feel that the subordinate's job is so unique as not to lend itself to the usual evaluation. These and many other rationalizations are given in order to escape the task of evaluating a subordinate. Behind them all may well be the fear of alienating the subordinate, the lack of sufficient verifiable evidence to make a judgment, the desire of the boss to focus on her own job rather than engage in unpleasant criticism of the subordinate's job, indifference, and the feeling on the part of managers that subordinates know intuitively how well they are doing without the need to press the matter further.

Nevertheless, performance appraisal as a system or a tool is here to stay. The company will continue to expect its middle managers to assess their human resources periodically. The professional manager will continue to regard performance appraisal, whether formal or informal, as a very useful tool. She will find it a valuable management tool not only in helping subordinates improve their present performance and become qualified for other responsible assignments, but also in making valid judgments about recommendations for promotion, advancement, transfer, or termination. Employees, too, will continue to insist upon performance appraisal as part of their bill of rights, which includes the right to be informed how they are doing, where they stand, what their strengths and weaknesses are, and how to rectify the latter, as well as the right to be assured that they are not victims of discriminatory action or, simply, personal dislike.

Whatever your appraisal system may be, formal or informal,

here are some important guidelines for you to follow in making your appraisal meaningful and productive. The guidelines are cited as the big C's below:

1. **Consistency.** Harmony with the codified statements of one's position, responsibilities and standards of performance.

2. **Confirmed Observation.** Checks on the results of work that are frequent enough, clear enough, and detailed enough to confirm your observations.

3. **Candid Discussion.** Joint discussion of strengths, weaknesses, problems, aspirations, and organizational impediments, if any.

4. **Constructive Criticism.** Criticism based on fair assessment of facts, events, and performance, enabling the subordinate to improve with a feeling of confidence and trust.

5. **Corrective Action.** Sound, timely, and feasible corrective measures taken as warranted throughout the year, not only during the formal annual appraisal period.

6. **Counseling.** Attitude of listening, guiding, advising, reinforcing, and challenging, but never permitting the employee to lean on his or her superior as a supportive crutch.

7. **Clarification.** Explanation of requirements, expectations, duties, systems, procedures, policies, rules as needed in dialogue with the employee.

8. **Capability Potential.** Continuing focus on the employee's potential in terms of skills, attitudes, outlook, competencies, team participation, aspirations, opportunities, so that as the employee's capability potential is realized, the capabilities of the department and the company are enhanced as well.

Follow-up will often be needed in moving toward improved performance, so it is well to chart what the subordinate can and will do for himself or herself, what you as the manager can do to expedite or accelerate improvement, and what the two of you can do jointly.

TRAINING, GUIDING, COACHING YOUR SUBORDINATES

We turn now to the specific task of developing human resources. This is not a new idea, of course. The notion of patronizing talent long predates the formal concept in administration theory. Editors have nurtured promising reporters, experienced physicians have tutored young interns, master craftsmen have taught their trade apprentices, learned clergymen have mentored newly ordained ministers of the faith, and successful jurists have taken budding attorneys in their law offices under their wing. In modern business, corporate concern for human resources in building competitive strength is prompting the demand that managers at all levels develop their subordinates in the state of the art, largely through on-the-job training in skills that are relevant to their functions. Although it is difficult to trace the origins of this concept in business (it may go back to the flourishing commerce in ancient China or to European mercantilism), the idea is generally believed to have assumed its modern form as a concept and technique with the emergence of the automotive and steel industries in the United States. In England, it presumably dates back to the thrust of the Industrial Revolution.

Its essence is one-to-one coaching on the job. As a trainer, guide, or coach, the professional manager can best meet this responsiblity by knowledge and application in these areas:

The factors that help people develop and grow.

The basic principles of the psychology of behavior and of the learning process.

The dynamics of coaching for individual development.

The various approaches used for total employee development.

WHAT MAKES PEOPLE GROW

Of the many attempts to research this question, the General Electric Company staff in charge of its management development program is credited with having developed what is probably the best statement of principles. GE's credo stresses these points:

The development process is a highly individual matter. What may be good for one person may not be good for another; the method that works well for one individual may not work well for another. Development, then, has to be tailored to fit the strengths and needs of the individual.

Every person's business development is self-development. Although the company may help, the effort and responsibility to develop and grow are mainly obligations of the individual employee.

Development of people cannot be based on any set of ideal personality characteristics or traits. Some people may be tough and aggressive while others are mild and thoughtful. The focus must be on the work, which can be observed, analyzed, and measured, and not on personality.

One's development is about 90 percent the result of day-to-day work experience. Specific experiences, contacts, relationships with the immediate superior, and the general working climate are the most potent influence in developing or retarding individual growth. Educational background, courses, and other exposures have only relatively minor impact on one's development.

Development opportunity must be universal. The chance to develop should be given to all, the promising and the unpromising. Variations can be made, however, in the nature of opportunities provided to those who are brighter and more highly motivated, as against those with limited abilities and incentive.

Primary emphasis should be on development in the present job, rather than on promotion. Improving one's performance in his or her present job must be the key concern. Overcoming weaknesses, building strengths, and learning new skills in the present job are primary. These will probably prove later to be assets. The company should encourage the worker to qualify himself or herself for advancement, but not at the expense of the present job.

Decentralization of decision-making is a prime development instrument. Decision-making ability in subordinates is developed only to the extent that they are enabled to make decisions. Decentralizing part of decision-making so that subordinates have an opportunity to take such responsibily is most significant.

Moral and spiritual values are basic to the development process. As the individual acquires more knowledge and influence, that person has an obligation to be right in the quality of decisions made, and particularly those involving people. Moral values must rank high in our relationships with people and in the social responsibilities which face us.*

One may add the important points that the boss and the climate she sets have a major influence on one's development; and, finally, that development is a continuing and often a long-term process, not an occasional encounter or a crash program.

The manager as guide must also be alert to the principal motivations that spark most subordinates to perform. They include the following: the feeling of *security*—financial and psychological—in one's job; the desire for *identity*—being accepted by peers, belonging, having friendships, working and sharing experiences with

*From Moorehead Wright, *What Makes a Manager Grow,* General Electric Company. Credit and permission of the Management Development Institute, General Electric Company, Croton-on-Hudson, New York.

others; the need for *participation and recognition*—to express oneself, take part in an effort, use one's skills and judgment, and be recognized for effective results; *ego needs*—independence of thought, self-assertion, use of expertise, use of authority, exercise of influence, esteem, status, enjoying well-earned prestige; the desire for *responsibility and challenge*—taking on additional obligations, meeting a challenge, solving a problem, representing others, originating new methods; and, general *self-fulfillment*—realizing ones potential. For subordinates in supervisory positions, of course, most of the same motivations can be translated into satisfactions sought in the supervisory role.

Finally, you must develop skill in identifying the "comers" or high achievers because of their special value as human resources. We have come to know more about these individuals and what makes them "tick." These are some of the relevant characteristics:

High achievers:

Seek responsibility, both official and personal.

Are willing to take risks—moderate and calculated risks.

Set tough goals for themselves—challenging but realistic goals.

Show high capability for setting up work plans for activities and prospective results.

Exhibit empathy for the responsibilities and problems of their superiors.

Seek candid, specific, measurable feedback on the results of their work, and can take criticism as well as praise. Moreover, they seek feedback that is prompt and unbiased.

Find satisfaction in a measure of freedom to pursue goals of their own choosing, within reason and consistent with the larger company goals.

Seek opportunities and responsibilities on which they can "make good" rather than be thwarted.

Feel that appropriate recognition and reward should be given for jobs well done.

Have a high energy level and can and will put in many hours and hard work.

Show emotional stability and can accept the pressures of the job and of other special assignments.

Give greater evidence of analytic abilities, judgment, and flexibility than do most other employees.

In tapping this valuable human resource, the manager will do well to recognize these characteristics and draw upon them.

THE ART OF COACHING

The good coach should know exactly what the subordinate needs to improve his or her work performance and why. The range of possibilities is quite extensive and it may include one or more of the following factors. These examples both specify the need and indicate what the manager can do about it. As coach, the manager can:

Help the subordinate make fewer errors and learn from and capitalize on these mistakes.

Enable the subordinate to handle more difficult tasks well.

Help the subordinate understand new information, new systems, and new procedures affecting his or her work.

Sharpen the employee's analytic abilities in identifying, probing, and solving problem situations.

Encourage the subordinate to make independent judgments and decisions, to stand on his or her own feet.

Develop the subordinates' oral and written communication skills on the job.

Sharpen the employee's sense of priorities, essentials, vital elements in the job situation.

Enhance the employee's technical competence in the specific function.

Improve the worker's abilities in relating with people in daily on-the-job situations.

Enable the subordinate to overcome blind spots, hangups, rigidity, and other personal impediments affecting job performance.

Encourage the subordinate to participate more actively in the department's problem-solving and decision-making process.

Advise the subordinate on using his or her time effectively.

Reassure the subordinates about risk-taking and decision-making as part of the nature of the business environment.

Contend with the employee's negative feelings, sense of discouragement, and self-doubts.

Bolster the employee's self-confidence in undertaking new and unfamiliar assignments.

Clarify for the subordinates whatever needs clarification with regard to duties, responsibilities, authority.

Help the subordinate to manage better the employees under his or her direct supervision.

In general, the manager should help the subordinate learn more, grow, work more cooperatively and more competently, and contribute more to the good of the department.

A number of guidelines are suggested for you as coach in dealing with your subordinate. You have the responsibility and authority to alert the subordinate to the fact that you are aware of the difficulties he or she is encountering; don't hesitate to use your authority. Try to time your guidance so that it is most appropriate and seems to fall in naturally with routine manager-subordinate consultation. Let your subordinate define the problem as he or she sees it, express his or her feelings and reactions, suggest approaches and solutions, and explain the reasoning behind them. After you have initiated the discussion of performance, and your subordinate has had a chance to vent his or her own feelings and views, you can move on with more rigorous questioning, analysis, criticism as warranted, and thence to joint discussion about possible next steps toward improvement. Do your part well as a listener. Listen fully, attentively, and evaluatively. With respect to all the above guidelines, provide an atmosphere of openness, understanding, and trust.

The next important guideline is to be perceptive. Through dialogue, nondirective questioning, and the use of case incidents try to determine the following: What is the subordinate's attitude toward you? Toward other coworkers? About the company as a whole? How dependent is he or she on you in order to do the job? Why this degree of dependency? What is the subordinate's awareness that his or her performance may have to change? What are the realistic possibilities of such change for the purpose of self-improvement? How determined the subordinate is to make the necessary change?

This perceptiveness is required, of course, for the more critical instances involving work performance, the need for significant improvement, and coaching for further development of the subordinate. For the many less serious problems that occur, and that fall within the mainstream of normal corrective action, such perceptiveness may not be required. Lesser problems can be handled in terms of the usual pattern of spotlighting a weakness, discussing how it can best be overcome, and agreeing to feasible measures for improvement.

Coaching and counseling obviously require personalization. It is important, however, to be concerned about the degree of personalization. A manager, even in the role of well-intentioned tutor or coach, is not a minister, parent, or physician to the subordinate. Provide an atmosphere of warmth, encouragement, openness, and understanding—but guard against buddyism, intimacy, personal analysis, or even innocent manipulation. Personal factors affecting a subordinate's performance may well arise in the dialogue, such factors as marital and family relations, health, deep emotional stress, career frustration, feelings of hostility, or personal finances. Listen and empathize, if you wish, but avoid extending the discussion further than suggesting possible sources of professional expertise. It is best, also, to cut off personalization if the motives, actions, and reputations of other coworkers are raised. The coach-subordinate discussion is a one-to-one relationship, not an occasion to assess the individuals who make up the department's staff. If, however, corrective action is required to improve a *working* relationship and for smoother and more efficient organizational functioning, that is another matter. In short, it is important for you as coach to show that you care enough about the individual's performance, growth, and career development to help him or her improve that performance. But in doing so, avoid the traps of overpersonalization.

Within the context of principles of teaching and learning and the general psychology of coaching, there are other guidelines. Start where the employee *is,* not where you wish him or her to be. Subordinates come to the job with different kinds of background, experience, interest, learning ability, and motivation. Begin where they are with respect to their skills and competencies, then proceed gradually and cumulatively, depending on evidence of performance and suitability of coaching. Try to teach only as much at one time as the employee can absorb. Some people understand more easily and quickly, others are harassed by work pressures and cannot think too clearly for an extended period, and still others are eager to take on as much tutoring as they can get. Don't confine yourself to oral explanation. Exhibits, cases, charts, reports, illustrations, and visual aids are often helpful in the teaching process. The effective coach also respects the time-honored maxim that people learn best by doing and provides opportunities to practice, repeat, analyze, decide, and solve problems. Involving the subordinate in *doing* reinforces the learning process. Bear in mind also the principle of individual differences. Subordinates differ in their strengths, weaknesses, aspirations, innate intelligence and ability to make judgments, capacity for taking criticism, and perceptions of the social process in which people work and act together. These differences influence their abilities to relate in the teaching-learning, superior-subordinate process as well.

Focus on improvement goals and follow up by observing progress made toward these goals. If you are dissatisfied with the rate of progress, repeat the coaching or some aspects of it as necessary. Keep enough distance to let the subordinate proceed independently and put new knowledge into practice. Expect mistakes on the part of the subordinate, but expect, too, that he or she demonstrate that something has been learned from these mistakes and that such errors will not recur.

As you engage in coaching, take other important guidelines into account. Subordinates should be regularly posted on new information, current findings, and plans. Set up a system for receiving regular progress reports from subordinates—weekly, biweekly, or monthly reports. Provide ample opportunity for each worker to think for himself or herself—in anticipating developments, seeking ways to improve the work situation, and working cooperatively. If there is uncertainty about someone's abilities, add responsibilities gradually and keep reinforcing the person's feeling for acceptance of responsibility. Be accessible to your subordinates and make them feel comfortable in asking questions and seeking clarification. Hold each subordinate accountable for the discharge of responsibilities and for actions and results. Criticize and discipline as situations warrant, but do so constructively and with confidence in improvement. See that subordinates know they must admit their mistakes promptly and then get on with the show. Brooding, expressing guilt or self-doubt, trying to escape by directing blame toward others, fearing risk in the future—none of these reactions is productive in dealing with mistakes once they have been made, and you should stress that point with subordinates.

The task of the guide is not easy. It requires large blocks of managerial time. There will inevitably be some failures along the way, people will not develop far enough or soon enough despite your coaching and counseling. It will not be easy to guide the man or woman who already feels sufficiently qualified but was recently passed up for promotion. Dealing with the chronically angry person is not a task to be relished. Nor is it easy in the organizational bureaucracy to "unhitch" people who are mismatched with their jobs. One distressing task is to give a subordinate supervisor the responsibilities of a supervisor when he or she is truly a technician, and evidently prefers that role. Obsolete pay scales are often a general damper on the desire of subordinates for self-improvement. An employee's distrust of top management generally may hinder that person's ability to trust you, despite the irrationality of such suspicion. Your own inexperience as a trainer and a counselor may reveal itself and impair the one-to-one relationship. At many points in the relationship, there may still be a need to order, warn, and engage in other directive action. Nevertheless, this managerial role should not jeopardize the basic relationship and a climate of commitment to developing subordinates.

The way to build a good team is to develop people individually, so that collectively they can reinforce your management of the department. To the extent that subordinates become self-sufficient in handling things well at their level, so will you, the manager, be released for more urgent priorities affecting the department. This is the road, too, to managerial succession in a company. It has been said that a manager is free to move just as fast and as far as his subordinates enable her to go. There may be much truth in it. If you are unable to recognize this interdependence between manager and subordinates, then you may well question your choice of management as a career.

OTHER DEVELOPMENTAL SOURCES

Other means are, of course, available to supplement on-the-job coaching. They can be used in various kinds of situations: when swift and radical changes are taking place in the technology or the state of the art, and the subordinates must be fully oriented; when one has been on the job too long, has lost interest and has gone stale; when the individual has to learn much more about his field to meet performance standards; when entirely new skills must be acquired; or when new demands and increasing interdependence require a better understanding of functions outside of his or her field. Other possibilities include training by other, more economical, means than direct supervisory guidance, and the availability of expertise from other quarters.

Managers are generally familiar with such supplementary developmental sources. A brief review lists some of the more important of these:

Outside seminars and conferences.

Committee, task force membership.

Rotation to other departments.

Guided reading in one's field.

Role-playing situations.

Exposure to business "games."

Formal courses.

Official travel to field posts.

Career counseling services.

Participation in organizational changes.

Designation as "acting" head.

Staff meeting attendance.

Membership in professional societies.

Special delegations.

Job redesign.

Performance review follow-up.

Manual revision assignments.

Involvement in planning guide for new systems.

The above, and other means of education and training, should be considered selectively to reinforce on-the-job training. However, direct on-the-job experience and coaching by the manager still constitute about 90 percent of the total development effort.

How-to Guidelines for the Trainer and Guide

1. Consult periodically with the personnel department on your projected staffing needs—both short- and long-term requirements.

2. Develop the needed skills for more effective interviewing and screening of candidates. Too high a price is paid for hiring the wrong people. To the extent possible, then, be most conscientious in assessing people before they are hired.

3. Review job specifications and the qualification requirements. Obsolescence may have taken place. Update both job specifications and required qualifications and keep them current.

4. Establish performance standards for every position reporting to you. Do it jointly with incumbents. Be willing to bend on legitimate points of difference. Revise the standards as conditions warrant.

5. Monitor your turnover rates. Review and diagnose the causes for voluntary resignations, terminations, early retirements, re-

quests for transfers, demotions, and other turnover. Seek help in trying to reduce undesired turnover. Human resources accounting reveals that the costs of turnover are high.

6. Comply with the company's formal appraisal system as much as possible, despite any reservations you may have. Follow through on the findings and observe changes for better or worse until the next appraisal period.

7. Conduct your own informal appraisals of employees' performance on a continuing basis. They will probably be valuable both for you and for your subordinates.

8. Provide a sound pattern for orienting or breaking in new employees in the department.

9. Review the job evaluations and salary levels for jobs in your department. Press to have these revised, if necessary, in order to attract and hold people with better qualifications.

10. Be people-conscious: know your people, size up their capabilities, show appreciation of their good work, give candid criticism of their poor work, and provide the kind of climate that will best tap their abilities, and that will be conducive to higher productivity.

11. Be on the alert for any technological displacement of human effort. Work closely with the personnel department in reducing the severity of the impact, maintaining good morale as much as possible under the circumstances, and in trying to salvage the best talent for retraining and placement elsewhere in the company.

12. Acknowledge the interdependence of manager and subordinates; each needs the other in modern organization. Stress mutuality: mutual concern, mutual responsibilities, and mutual accomplishments.

13. Be accessible to your people, communicate clearly, in time, and regularly. Let them know in advance of things which may af-

fect them on the job, be a good listener, and provide them with useful feedback from which they can benefit and improve in performance.

14. Recommend dropping dead wood from the payroll. Marginal workers, incompetents, chronic malcontents who are disruptive of team effort and departmental output, and others should, after discussion and sufficient opportunity to change, be terminated. Be sure, however, that this is your honest judgment and that they are not worthy of retention either in your department or in the company.

15. Make a commitment to invest in your people. Invest to train, guide, coach, and counsel for their continuing growth. The investment will often pay off the efficiency of the department as well. Keep your commitment. Do not blow hot and cold in this respect, for it may affect your credibility with your subordinates.

16. Exercise patience. It takes time and patience to achieve the level of competence and degree of contribution you want from your subordinates.

17. Recognize and reward people for superior accomplishment, originality, resourcefulness, and creative effort in behalf of the department, with financial and nonfinancial rewards.

18. Strive for credibility with your subordinates. Keep promises, provide opportunities equitably, back workers when they deserve it, respect confidences, acknowledge mistakes, and show consistency in your personnel actions.

19. Be tough-minded in your expectations of performance. Show your displeasure and reject shoddy work, the weak presentation, the unreasoned decision, the mediocre job. Expect *more* of your people, and they will generally stretch to meet the demands placed upon them.

20. Be neither too lenient nor too severe in rating your subordinates in the official appraisal system. Just be fair and candid.

21. Know the morale of your subordinates as a group, If there are signs of lowered morale, diagnose the situation and take measures as soon as possible to restore morale to a higher level. Although there may be academic debate in the management field about the correlation between morale and productivity, the body of experience and seasoned observation testifies that poor morale *does* have an adverse effect on a group's productivity.

22. Be sure of your ground when recommending people for lateral transfer, advancement, or promotion. And when you're sure, do it with full endorsement and with a strong vote of confidence in their continued growth as "comers" in the organization.

23. Do not mourn the loss of a superior employee, though you may regret having to see that person go. Start a search for the best possible replacement. The fact is that both you and the department have probably gained more in three years of service from this superior employee than in ten years with a mediocre worker. Consider what you have gained rather than what you are about to lose.

24. Set a high example of ethical and moral behavior.

25. If and when you finally must move on elsewhere, take pride in having left behind for the company a legacy of talented and high-caliber subordinates whom you helped to develop. It may be that you have even developed your own successor.

Self-Audit: Are You a Good Trainer and Guide?

When my subordinate encounters "rough waters" in the daily managerial job, I generally

____ let him or her ride it out alone, to sink or swim.　　( )

____ promptly try to give him or her a hand with the problem, if I can.　　( )

____ break in only when he or she asks for my advice or assistance.　　( )

When the reports my employee submits to me are less than satisfactory, I

____ kick it back with a memo, "You can do better than this."　　( )

____ try to edit and improve it myself, if I find the time, rather than interrupt the job he or she is on at the time.　　( )

____ call the person in, identify the weak spots in the report, listen to any rebuttal, and suggest another crack at it.　　( )

When my subordinate's attitudes toward people seem to irritate them, I generally

____ chalk it up to personality and let nature take its course, hoping that more experience in dealing with people will change him or her.　　( )

____ try to act as peacemaker, and assure the people that he or she really didn't intend to offend them.　　( )

____ report the incident to that person, discuss it, and let my subordinate do what he or she wants about it.　　( )

When my worker stalls in making a decision on a problem awaiting solution, I generally

_____ don't worry about it
the delay is his or her risk
and responsibility. ( )

_____ urge him or her to decide on it
before things get worse
or out of hand. ( )

_____ call a meeting to discuss it
but then let the employee
make his or her own
decision. ( )

When he or she takes on a trouble-shooting assignment for me, I generally

_____ get the word around to those
concerned and leave it to
him or her from there on. ( )

_____ wait until the troubleshooting job is over, and
then pass judgment on how
well it was done. ( )

_____ confer from time to time
to check on progress made,
and problems he or she is
encountering. ( )

When he appears to be bungling a delegation on a special project, I generally

_____ withdraw the delegation
before he or she gets
in any further. ( )

_____ let the person see it
through in the hope that he or
she will learn from
mistakes. ( )

_____ intercede to check on possible
misunderstanding and to see
if he or she
can get back on the
target assignment. ( )

203

Self-Audit (continued)

When I observe that he or she is not using managerial time wisely, I generally

_____ wait until a deadline is missed or an important item neglected and then criticize him or her. ( )

_____ break in to remind him or her of the difference between priorities and routine matters, or what to act on and what to defer. ( )

_____ point up my observations and try to teach him or her how to budget time more effectively as a manager, since time is money. ( )

When he or she comes up with an idea about which I'm unenthusiastic, I generally

_____ brush it off and tell him or her it's best not to rock the boat. ( )

_____ go through the motions of forwarding it up to my boss or others concerned and with no endorsement on my part. ( )

_____ discuss it candidly, get the person to think it over, and encourage him or her to try again; I don't squelch any idea germination. ( )

When my subordinate is working away at a sound organizational change for the department, I generally

_____ let him or her hide away to finish the project and the whole package. ( )

_____ check with my superiors to let them know what's "in works" as a management improvement. ( )

_____ advise the person to work on it but to involve his or her people for their participation and suggestions at the same time. ( )

When my subordinate appears to be running a "one-person show," in supervising his or her own unit of workers, I generally

_____ allow freedom to "make or break" as he or she sees fit. ( )

_____ alert the person to the consequences on the morale of his or her people that might result from this behavior. ( )

_____ discuss ways to get more get more productivity out of the unit through better use of their talents so that he or she will havemore time to spend on priority management items. ( )

Score: If your answers are largely in the first column, you are not doing well in developing your human resources. If your answers are mainly in the middle column, you tend to blow hot and cold but are still not doing well in dealing with your subordinates. If your answers are for the most part in the third column, with only about one or two in the middle one, credit yourself with developing your subordinates quite effectively.

Appendix

Elements of Managing

ELEMENTS OF MANAGING

The management of industrial, governmental, church, and military institutions and other types of enterprises proceeds, for the most part, under the same sequence of elements and processes. The management skills attained in one field should, in most cases, be transferable to another.

Management is a leadership effort aimed at integrating and using effectively the many resources entrusted to the manager: people, money, facilities, relationships, ideas, time, equipment, and other assets. It must be guided by established objectives, and it must achieve a balance of management functions in attaining these objectives.

A manager is responsible, within his or her organizational unit, for the key elements and processes of management as outlined below.

PLANNING

Planning includes:

1. Establishing and interpreting goals and objectives.

2. Formulating and issuing policies which are, in effect, standing management decisions.

3. Establishing programs—that is, those functions and activities to be pursued in reaching the defined goals through the guiding policies.

4. Providing the components needed in order to fulfill the goal and the programs planned: people, money, material, time, facilities, ideas, and other resources necessary for moving ahead effectively.

5. Developing expectations and timetables which are subsequently refined into standards and schedules.

6. Differentiating between short- and long-range plans, standing plans and interim plans, and other distinctions in the total planning function.

7. Determining who is to represent the organization in the formulation and revision of plans.

ORGANIZING

Organizing should provide:

1. Alignment of major functions and the proper structuring of departments, divisions, and other functional and structural units in the organization.

2. Delineation of the responsibilities, authority, and accountability of key positions.

3. A sound division of labor and specialization.

4. System for communication, coordination, and reporting.

5. Staffing with the necessary people for the management, supervisory, specialization, technical, clerical, maintenance, and other roles to perform the functions.

6. Preparation of manuals, position descriptions, administrative handbooks, and other tools to clarify and make known the conferring of responsibilties, authority, and accountability of those to whom functions are assigned.

7. Clarification of delegated authority.

8. Formal and informal organization.

9. A network of relationships, particularly, line and staff relations, and headquarters-field relations.

10. Committees, survey groups, task forces, and other special group units.

11. A framework susceptible to change in periods of stress or growth.

COORDINATING

Coordinating attempts to achieve:

1. Balance in the set of relationships established.

2. Communication channels among people in order to check and verify or obtain clearance and authorization.

3. Systematic means for bringing together the organization's resources and functional specializations into an integrated whole.

4. Exchange of views, ideas, and information; better understanding; plans.

5. Appropriate review and consultation.

Focus is on balance, collaboration, problems, integration, compatibility.

MOTIVATING

Motivating involves:

1. An understanding of what makes people "tick" in an enterprise—motivations.

2. Alertness to the basic and special needs and interests of workers whose reasonable fulfillment leads to job satisfaction.

3. Ability to gauge evidence of dissatisfaction leading to grievances, complaints, absenteeism, poor communication, turnover, and other manifestations of poor morale.

4. The provision of structure, processes, and opportunities conducive to good employee morale.

5. Incentives—and the assessment of their effectiveness.

6. Productivity and the individual employee.

7. Intelligent selection and placement and a sound compensation system.

8. Means of recognition and reward.

9. Counseling, appraising, coaching, and training in the development of subordinates.

DIRECTING

Directing is featured by organizing plus:

1. Installing, launching, and implementing the programs which have been planned and for which an organizational base has been established.

2. Operating the programs through systems, procedures, processes, and other means designed for them.

3. Making adjustments in staffing, as necessary or desirable.

4. Developing rules, regulations, requirements, and guides for effective operations.

5. Supervising operations to ensure full utilization of people, money, materials, facilities and other resources with minimum

of waste and with concern for qualitative and quantitative performance reviews.

6. Communicating with upper levels of management as necessary to resolve certain problems.

7. Requiring reports and other means of accountability.

8. Enforcing rules and regulations.

CONTROLLING

Controlling requires:

1. Devising performance standards.

2. Establishing measurable means for gauging adequacy of use of resources or performance of functions.

3. Devising systems for determining the extent to which developed standards are being met and, if they are not met, the extent of deviation from the standards.

4. Recording and evaluating the completed work—that is, reviewing.

5. Serving, in general, for feedback of information and findings which are useful to managers in taking corrective action to improve situations.

The Manager's Job*

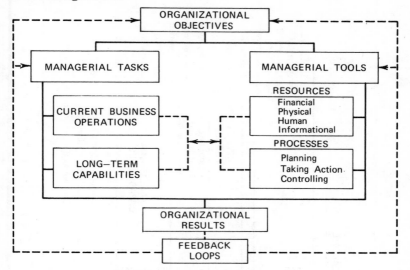

*Adapted from the *Michigan Business Review,* July 1970.

The Manager's Job*

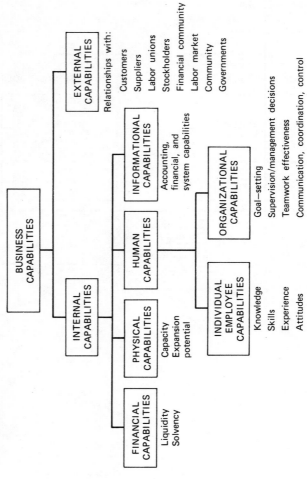

BUSINESS CAPABILITIES

- **INTERNAL CAPABILITIES**
  - **FINANCIAL CAPABILITIES**
    - Liquidity
    - Solvency
  - **PHYSICAL CAPABILITIES**
    - Capacity
    - Expansion potential
  - **HUMAN CAPABILITIES**
    - **INDIVIDUAL EMPLOYEE CAPABILITIES**
      - Knowledge
      - Skills
      - Experience
      - Attitudes
    - **ORGANIZATIONAL CAPABILITIES**
      - Goal–setting
      - Supervision/management decisions
      - Teamwork effectiveness
      - Communication, coordination, control
  - **INFORMATIONAL CAPABILITIES**
    - Accounting, financial, and system capabilities
- **EXTERNAL CAPABILITIES**
  - Relationships with:
    - Customers
    - Suppliers
    - Labor unions
    - Stockholders
    - Financial community
    - Labor market
    - Community
    - Governments

*Adapted from the *Michigan Business Review*, July 1970.

The Levels of Management—and the Responsibilities and Functions at Each Level (Critical "Make or Break" Elements at Each Level)

TOP EXECUTIVE ROLE
(Emphasis)
Conceptualization
Leadership
Resources
Assessment

Establishing management philosophy and objectives
Forecasting and goal-setting
Planning (broad, long-range) as well as early and intermediate
Policy formulation
Executive control
Resources "investment"
Organizational planning
Representation
And so on

Issues and decisions
Selection of key officers
Public relations
Financial risk
Control
Assessment
Integration of multiple functions

MIDDLE MANAGEMENT ROLE
(Emphasis)
Program development
Interpretation
Decision-making
Coordination
Reporting

Planning—short-term, intermediate
Implementation and follow-through on policy determinations
Staff work on policy guidance
Functional responsibility—technical excellence
Interpretation; communication
Organizational effectiveness
Decision-making
Monitorship and control: return on investment
Program planning and priorities
Coordination
And so on

Direction, coordination, and control
Evaluation of progress and reporting
Selection and development of supervisors
Standards of supervisory performance
Consultation, decisions

SUPERVISORY ROLE
(Emphasis)
Production
Reporting
Employee training

Work assignments; measurement of results
Technical direction of work
Standards of performance
Systems and procedures
Work improvement measures
Employee discipline and morale
Cost control, economies
Motivation and development of employees
And so on

Rules and regulations
Orders, instructions
Manuals of procedures
Union contract compliance
Physical environment (safety, efficiency)

215

Selected Readings

Basil, Douglas C.
Women in Management. Dunnellen, 1972.

Bird, Caroline
Women: Opportunity for Management. President's Association (Special Study No. 53), American Management Associations, 1973.

Bower, Marvin
The Will to Manage. McGraw-Hill, 1966.

Brenner, Marshall H.
Management Development for Women. *Personnel Journal,* March 1972.

Broad, Mary
Developing Women's Resources. *Training and Development Journal,* September 1975.

Cribbin, James J.
Effective Managerial Leadership. AMACOM, American Management Association, 1972.

Drucker, Peter F.
The Effective Executive. Harper & Row, 1967.

Drucker, Peter F.
Management: Tasks, Responsibilities, Practices. Harper & Row, 1974.

Ewing, David W.
The Managerial Mind. Free Press, 1964.

217

Gordon, Francine and Strober, Myra H.
Bringing Women into Management. McGraw-Hill, 1975.

Hennig, Margaret and Jardin, Anne
The Managerial Woman. Anchor, 1977.

Higginson, Margaret and Quick, Thomas
The Ambitious Woman's Guide to a Successful Career. AMACOM,
American Management Associations, 1975.

Kanter, Rosabeth Moss
Men and Women of the Corporation. Basic Books, 1977.

Katz, Robert
Skills of an Effective Administrator. *Harvard Business Review.*
January- February 1955.

Lopez, F.M.
The Making of a Manager. American Management Associations,
1970.

Loring, Rosalind and Wells, Theodora
Breakthrough: Woman into Management. Van Nostrand Reinhold,
1972.

Lynch, Edith M.
The Executive Suite: Feminine Style. AMACOM, American Management Associations, 1973.

Mintzberg, Henry
The Managerial Job: Folklore and Fact. *McKinsey Quarterly,* Spring
1976.

Orth, Charles D. and Jacobs, Frederic
Women in Management: Pattern for Change. *Harvard Business
Review,* July-August 1971.

Reif, William et al.
Exploding Some Myths About Women Managers. *California
Management Review,* Summer 1975.

Schwartz, Eleanor B. and Rago, James J.
Beyond Tokenism: Women as True Corporate Peers. *Business
Horizons,* December 1973.

Stead, Bette Ann
Women in Management. *Vital Speeches of the Day,* July 15, 1975.

Stewart, Nathaniel
Strategies of Managing for Results. Parker, 1966.

Trotter, Virginia Y.
   Women in Leadership and Decision-Making. *Vital Speeches of the Day,* April 1, 1975.
Wells, Theodora
   Equalizing Advancement between Women and Men. *Training and Development Journal,* August 1973.
Wortman, Max S. Jr. and Sperling, Joann
   Defining the Manager's Job. AMACOM, American Management Associations, 1975.